TYPOGRAPHICS1

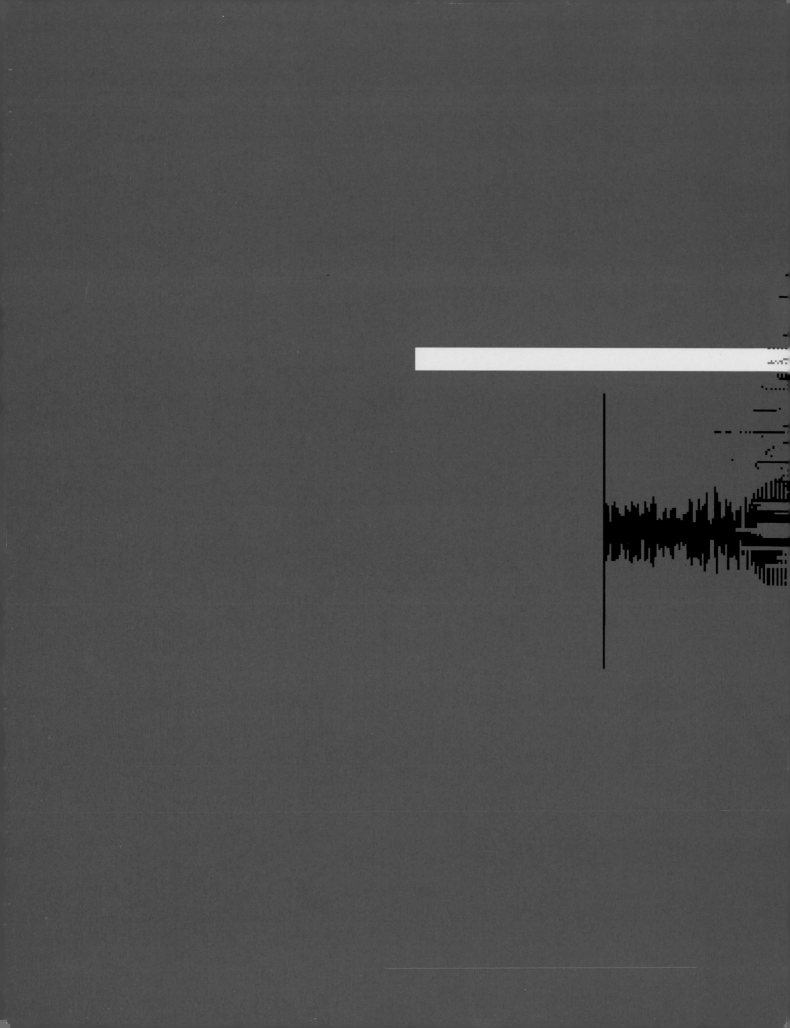

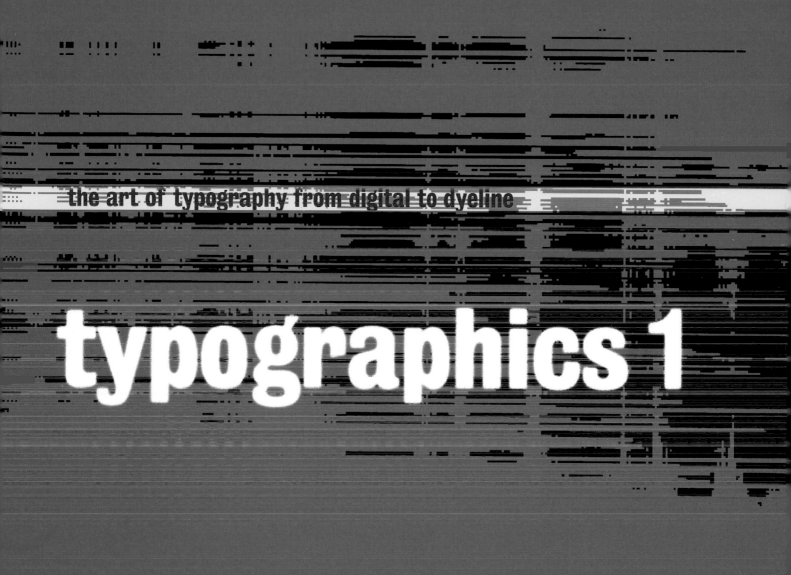

the art of typography from digital to dyeline

typographics 1

General Editor: Roger Walton

Typographics 1
First published by Hearst Books International,
1350 Avenue of the Americas, New York, NY
10019, United States of America
Distributed in North America by North Light
Books, an imprint of F & W Publications, Inc.,
1507 Dana Avenue, Cincinnati, OH 45207
1-800/289-0963

USA ISBN 0-688-15066-7

First published in Germany by:
NIPPAN
Nippon Shuppan Hanbai
Deutschland GmbH
Krefelder Str. 85
D-40549 Düsseldorf
Telephone: (0211) 5048089
Fax: (0211) 5049326

German ISBN 3-910052-89-4

Edited and Designed by
Duncan Baird Publishers
Castle House
75–76 Wells Street
London W1P 3RE

Designer: Karen Wilks
Editor: Lucy Rix

10 9 8 7 6 5 4 3 2 1

Typeset in Rotis Sans Serif
Color reproduction by Colourscan, Singapore
Printed in Hong Kong

NOTE: Dimensions for spread formats are single
page measurements; all measurements are for
width followed by height.

ENDPAPERS: A dyeline by Graham Wood, Tomato

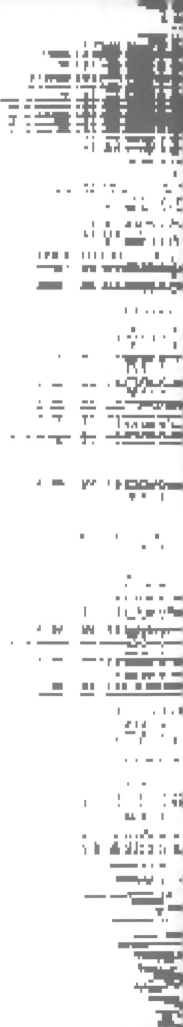

FOREWORD

Typographics 1 is the first volume in a series that will bring together recent examples of innovative, experimental, and outstanding work from professional and student typographers. The book is divided into four categories:

Type as Composition, showing designs that use minimal quantities of text;

Type Plus, the alliance of type and imagery;

Type as Text, compositions based on continuous text;

Type Itself, featuring recent font designs.

The aim of the book is not only to generate inspiration and promote debate, but also to focus attention on the current state of typography. The selection of work, made from over 1,000 submissions, was a difficult but rewarding task – the final choice represents the tremendous range and diversity of contemporary design.

In recent years, advanced technology and changing economic conditions have had a profound impact on the teaching and practice of typography. The widespread use of computers has brought about a significant increase in the number of self-initiated publications, many examples of which are shown here. The production costs of a modest publication seem now to be within the reach of the many rather than the few. This, alongside the imaginative use of digital technology and a wide range of printing processes, has generated a wonderful diversity of material. The work included in this book has been reproduced using litho presses, letter-press printing, silk-screen printing, color xeroxing, monochrome xeroxing, the fax machine, and dyeline processing.

Designers currently enjoy the luxury of access to highly sophisticated technology as well as to older printing and production techniques. It may be that this diversity will be short-lived as the older tools gradually become obsolete. There is, for example, only one design in this book that was originated entirely on a manual typewriter. The authentic typewriter typeface, with all its eccentricities and imperfections, and its connotations of journalistic urgency, is just one form of typographic language that will soon disappear. But the replacement of mechanical techniques by electronic processes does not necessarily restrict creativity or limit choice. Digital technology opens up new possibilities for the designer: typeface development, the positioning and repositioning of the elements of a design, the sourcing and manipulation of images, and the unprecedented speed with which change can be effected, combine in the new environment in which today's designers work. The dramatic pace of technological change also ensures that new techniques are discovered daily – by the time this book is printed, the software with which it was created will already have been modified.

Future editions of **Typographics** will continue to focus on changing trends in design and will draw on an even broader range of sources. As technological developments further influence typography, and as older traditions are reassessed and reappropriated, the most inspiring results will be celebrated here.

R.W.

type as composition

type as composition

designer
Dirk van Dooren

design company
Tomato

country of origin
UK

work description
Typo-psalm, a page from
Jetset magazine

dimensions
268 x 345 mm
10½ x 13⅝ in

designer
Nick Bell

art director
David Smart

design company
Nick Bell

13

country of origin
UK

work description
(1) cover visuals for
Decca records, using
multi-printed litho press
set-up sheets that allude
to the layered nature of
Ives' music

dimensions
120 x 120 mm
4¾ x 4¾ in

designer
Melle Hammer

design company
Plus X

country of origin
The Netherlands

work description
Case binding of the book
Een Vaste Vriend, for
Contact Publishers

dimensions
shown actual size
128 x 190 mm
5 x 7½ in

designer
Irma Boom

design company
Irma Boom

country of origin
The Netherlands

work description
Card-coverings from *The Spine*, publications bound together to form a single volume, published by De Appel Foundation

dimensions
300 x 210 mm
11⅞ x 8¼ in

designers
Mario A. Mirelez
Jim Ross

art director
Mario A. Mirelez

design company
Mirelez/Ross Inc.

country of origin
USA

work description
Exhibition catalog cover,
for the Herron Gallery

dimensions
280 x 227 mm
11 x 8⁷⁄₈ in

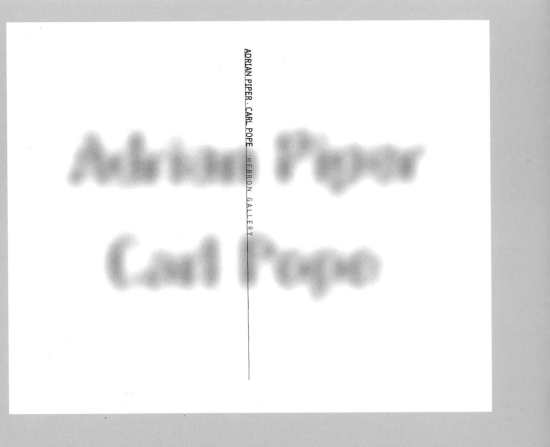

designer
Robbie Mahoney

college
Central Saint Martin's
College of Art and Design,
London

country of origin
UK

work description
Spreads from an
experimental magazine

dimensions
445 x 297 mm
17½ x 11¾ in

John Zorn

My background was mostly classical, studying composition, and through that I went towards improvisation - through having performers mess up my pieces to the extent that I felt I should do them myself, and have them realised in such a way that they couldn't be messed up.

Were you playing saxophone in those pieces?

I've only been playing saxophone six years now, so the pieces I did before then I didn't play at all. One of my main things has been combining theatre with music, and my early works were really about that - having people performing simple events as musical events. Getting up a ladder and peeling a cabbage or putting a tea pot to boil. The early ones were theatrical events that produced sounds - the sounds they produced I would orchestrate in a certain way, and the visual aspect was just something else again. And then I got more interested in eliminating the sound from those pieces and having just the theatrical events themselves, but no longer theatrical but musical - a visual musical event. The extension of that became the elimination of people performing those events, so that it was just the objects themselves as musical events.

I have a series of compositions, "The Theatre of Musical Optics", where I just have sets of objects which I arrange in different orders, with different timings and different combinations and that constitutes a musical piece. I feel that I'm coming out of a more composed area, a more classical area, while you've said you felt you came from more of a folk area. Is that where you guys are coming from?

I was just drawing a parallel between what we do and folk music. As far as my personal history is concerned, it was classical piano from the age of eight, classical trumpet from the age of fifteen, then playing in pop groups and soul groups...

But that involved improvising, right?

Yes.

So you've been improvising for a long time!

It was not until I first heard Cecil Taylor that I thought "Mhmm, I think I could do that" - and then realised very quickly that you can't just do that straight away.

The first thing I did on an instrument was improvise - playing the guitar first, and later the piano. I had to find something that was simple enough so that I could play something in that mode.

Something written you mean?

No, I was trying to play like Cecil Taylor and Monk, but I didn't understand jazz chords at all. Then I heard things like Booker T and the MGs, and they were using very simple chords, so I could see what was happening. I started from there. That is how I started improvising freely at the beginning.

To me, these early attempts at trying to imitate Monk or Taylor are just as much improvising as what you are doing now.

Absolutely, but it's a question of whether you feel helpless in that situation or not. Maybe you'd have a way of hearing what you're doing which could allow you to extend it, but at that point I didn't have that way of hearing it, it just sounded like shit to me.

But you must have enjoyed what you were doing.

Oh no, I hated it. I enjoyed playing classical music - but then I couldn't play without a score in front of me.

Really?

I had a complete block.

It's never had that. When I first started playing an instrument I was happy with what I was doing and I think thats the only reason I continue to play - not because I had a vision in my mind that this is where I'm going to be in five or ten years, but because I'm happy with what I was doing right then. Now I can listen back to the tapes and say, Well, they sound like shit - but at that time, maybe because my ears weren't that good, I thought what I was doing sounded great. I got a big kick out of it, and in that sense improvising has always been really strong for me, maybe because my ear hasn't been that good.

---

other places

Music has a pervasive and ambiguous influence. It enters lives as best it may. On there are those who say music has no meaning. They point to an Ab and say that there is no correspondence of this sound to a specific idea. They are right just as there is no meaning to the verbal sound "A". Just as every inflection of a mixture has a limited significance until it has been combined within a potent formula. The mixture tells us wether or not the parts are volatile or inert. Despite the fact that two notes - or two sounds immediately call for some inner response and analysis in the listener, and when even whole symphonies are full of colliding and coalescing sounds, some will say that it means nothing except...

And the consumption of a particular experience must in some way be mediated to make sense of it. No meanings arise from our needs and appetites. Music is more generally institutionalised and more amorphous that most other cultural phenomena. Meaning develops in music as listeners test and retest responses to it. Most of these understandings are taught, by example, by the currency of peer group recognition. Many often comprehend music in the same way that a musician has to. Music often understand musicians lose their love of music due to a surfeit of listening and to an over-familiarisation of repetitive recordings.

In terms of the aural beauty or otherwise of the construction, interpretation and the even human capacity to dance to it, there is a limit to the meaning of the music is inevitably bound up with complex cultural configuration. What is the culture moves people to tears on a banal and incomprehensible to another. Meaning is clearly attached to a collective understanding maybe induced by education or social conditioning - of what responses are appropriate to the conditioning of music. Those questions in question. These responses are learned and become reinforced by the literature, the critical mores, of the time. This generalised perception surely arises when a surfeit of musical meaning needs to be redressed.

Musicological and music critics are notorious for being led on with a relish. But their professionalism allows them to measure how well a piece is executed and even the craft value of old skill inside a performance causes more ordinary mentors. There is always a definition that meaning is conscious, that which attaches meaning in duration. We only often attribute correlation of beneficial meaning, or the perception that which is conscious, that which attaches meaning in duration. We only often attribute correlation of beneficial meaning, or the perception that which is power, moves the listener to a greater aesthetic response or insulation of good and bad are replaced by a catalogue of possible meanings, all of which must be based on a combination of human musicological and the conditioning to man in practice it is the free improvising musician who is more likely to heed this raw perceptual route. As my late colleague Bernidino Bacceat wrote in his essay "Towards an Ethic of Improvisation".

There will be a resultant part of his emerging being, with which the musician must live and progress from - note to note, performance to performance. It is this implicit experimentation that is the most significant philosophical difference between improvisation and the classical mode. The idea of the perfect form cannot be posited by the improviser for it destroys his creative stimuli. And no camouflage, passing the perfect solution, as we musicians are not at all familiar with each other's language, can ease dilemma. The relationship of an arrangement cannot be perfected by symmetry of ignorance. As much evolves between listening musicians than dialogue determines musical direction, even if the other parties try hard to ignore the other. Even in itself the perverse philosophy of improvisation inevitably has to deal with responses of some kind and new.

Other windows

The musician might want to turn it upside down or link it to other phenomena. The originality may transcend its initial impulse. No sound can ever be repeated. The condition of all musics are different everytime. Improvisation differs from other musics by using temporality and transience. Each moment in time is precious and original and the meta-musician celebrates and signifies this basic truth in performance. Improvised music is not a pastime. It upsets notions of music as leisure and music as something to be consumed, because it fixes on the unrelenting 'now' and is a means of self-realization, not an escape from reality.

The integrity of improvisation depends wholly upon the manner of its execution. A listener cannot be certain if a premeditated configuration is composed, freely improvised or some hybrid, unless it is a well-known piece that can be followed note for note. Such difficulties refer to all musics, even the more abstract and more heavily subscribed formulations.

The apocryphal story of the English troubadour Paul Rutherford comes to mind. On completing a performance of Berio's 'Sequenza for Trombone', Rutherford was rapturously congratulated. A listener informed him that he had never heard it played better. This was no real surprise to the musician because after a few moments of playing the score he had improvised the remaining music. An expected consequence of the integrity of an improvisation is musicians not repeating themselves. In reality they do and they don't. An improvising musician's identity arises out of certain continuities - of tuning, timbre, manner of phrasing and a whole range of habitual responses and personal predilections. These are the trail marks by which we can come to know a musical personality. The theoretical problem is whether these constitute an informal composition which thereby invalidates the aesthetic priority of improvisation. Such analysis will depend upon the definition and the meaningfulness of the term 'original'. A musician may make one original material or conceptual discovery in his whole career. Its development and exposition may consume most of his life.

Leisure is the anodynic observer to alienated labour which sublimates the subject. Activity is its reward; ourselves in it reality. Our being manifests itself in one of the myriad of possibilities for our decision to do. How satisfactory this is depends upon the emergent character we are becoming. Music, like life, is the vehicle we have for realizing the inner image we have of the world and our place in it. Music is never an end in itself. It is to the extent and too important to be crystallized. It is a living process. In making music we make ourselves.

This realisation is work enough for many life times. And the meta-musician weaves his way through the emergent strands of the object/subject dichotomy, always testing and teasing the very meaning of material existence. It is this attitude and general ethos that ultimately marks out the improviser. In heurism and dialogue the meta-musician is working towards a composition that will never be completed - although moments and realisations of satisfaction will occur, along with disappointment and irritation.

It is not enough for audiences to extract some tasty morsels. They are not there to be entertained. They are part of an important occasion. Musicians and audiences are there on serious business which of course need not be without humour and joy. The meta music is setting out potential parameters, laying out a kind of blueprint for new kind of human relationships. The meta musicians are like mandated delegates. The audience must be mindful of individual predilections, be intent upon relishing the unexpected and savour the technical prowess of the meta-music. They must become more and more concious that the dream-like qualities of the music - its sometimes weird and unpredictable shapes, its ability to twist the mind and the ear to new anticipations - are like windows on a world in which one would rather live. The meta-musician is at the heart of an experiment. The audience checks the validity of the results.

designer
André Baldinger

college
Atelier National de
Création Typographique,
Paris

country of origin
France

work description
Poster for the Atelier
National de Création
Typographique

dimensions
274 x 410 mm
10¾ x 16⅛ in

18

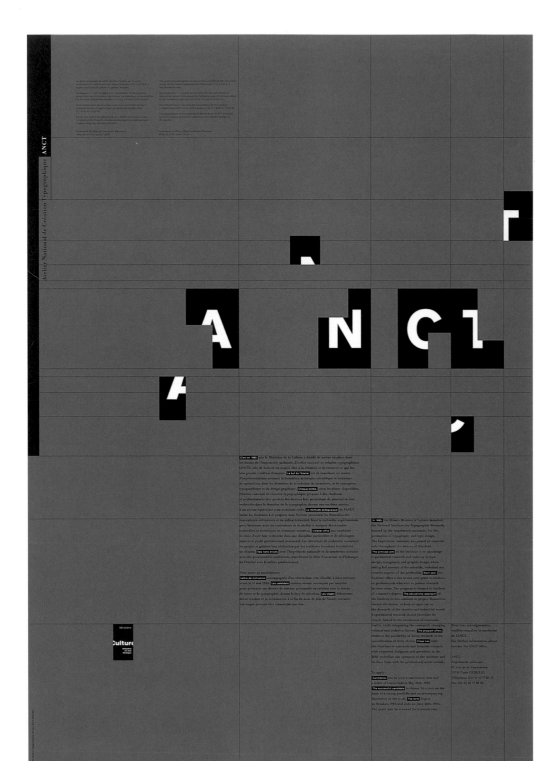

**Broadcast
Design
Software**

designer
Michael Renner

photographer
Michael Renner

design company
Michael Renner Design

country of origin
Switzerland

work description
*Broadcast Design
Software*, a poster for
Adobe Systems Inc.

dimensions
905 x 1275 mm
35⅝ x 50 in

designer
Irma Boom

design company
Irma Boom

country of origin
The Netherlands

work description
Case binding from an
exhibition catalog, *Round
Transparency, Marian
Bijlenga 1993*

dimensions
198 x 198 mm
7¾ x 7¾ in

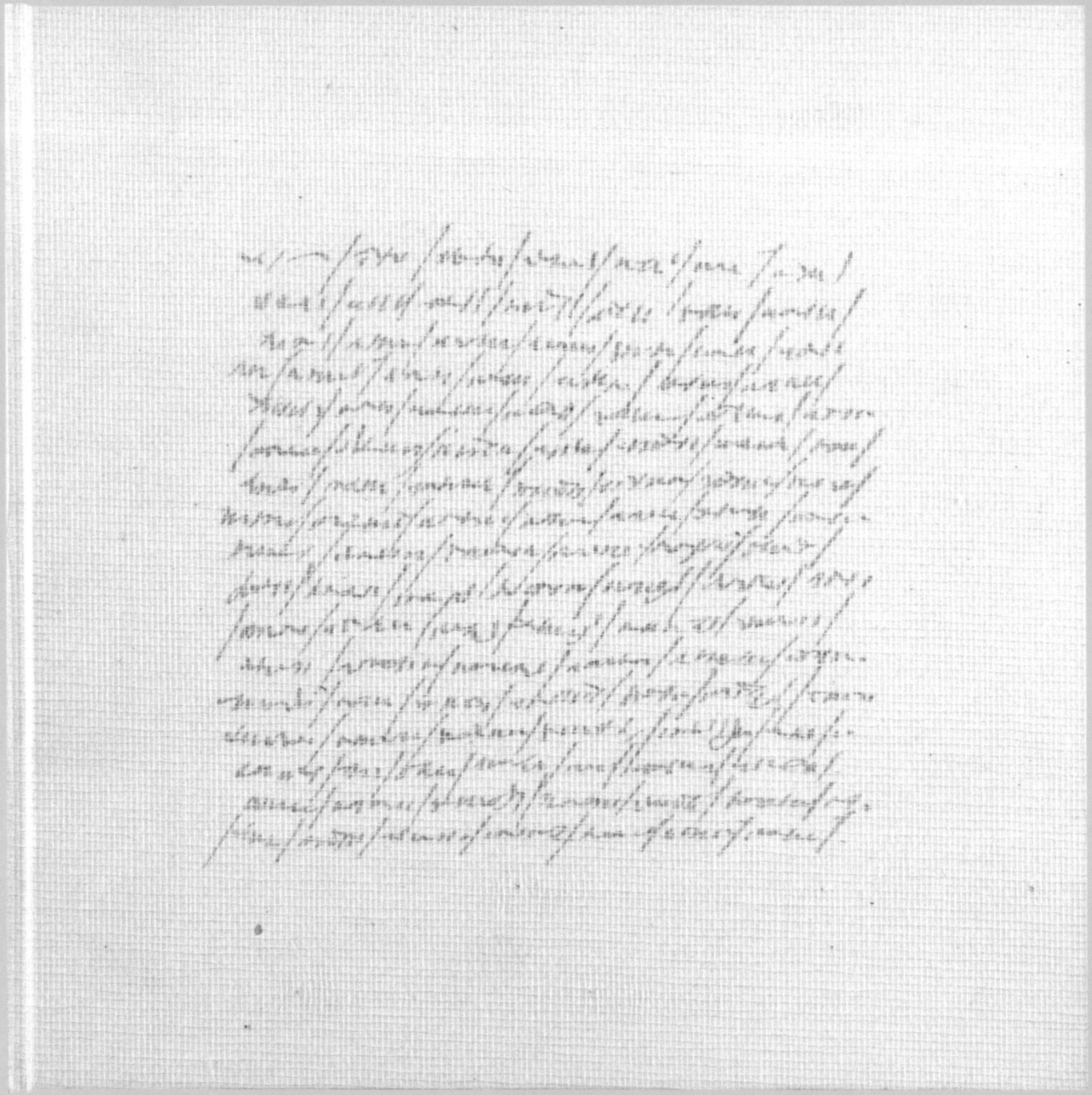

designer
Irma Boom

design company
Irma Boom

photographer
Ido Menco

country of origin
The Netherlands

work description
Case binding from an
exhibition catalog, *Tomas
Rajlich*

dimensions
161 x 208 mm
6⅜ x 8¼ in

TOMAS

RAJLICH

designer
Willi Kunz

design company
Willi Kunz Associates

country of origin
USA

work description
Lecture series posters for
Columbia University,
Graduate School of
Architecture, Planning,
and Preservation, New
York

dimensions
304 x 610 mm
12 x 24 in

22

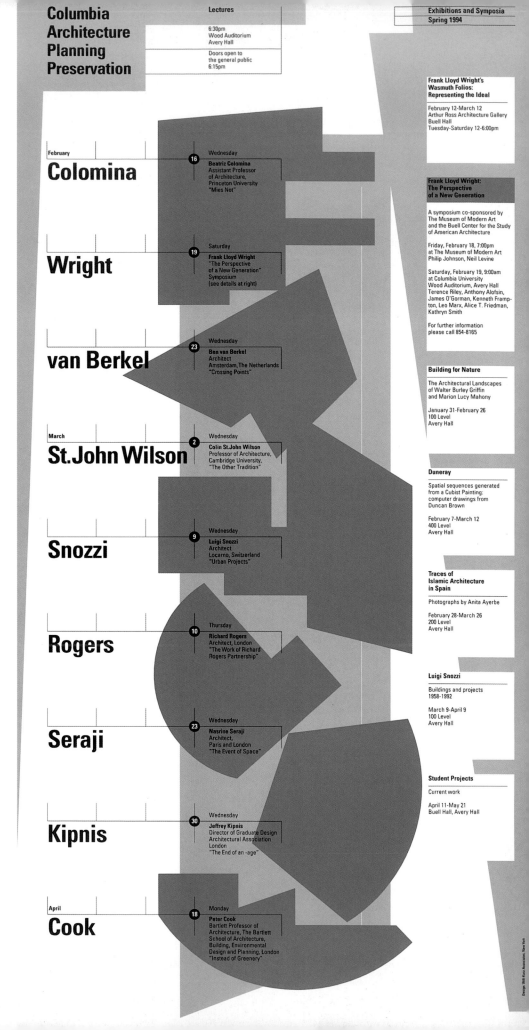

Columbia
Architecture
Planning
Preservation

Lectures

6:30pm
Wood Auditorium
Avery Hall

Doors open to
the general public
6:15pm

Exhibitions and Symposia
Spring 1994

**Frank Lloyd Wright's
Wasmuth Folios:
Representing the Ideal**

February 12-March 12
Arthur Ross Architecture Gallery
Buell Hall
Tuesday-Saturday 12-6:00pm

**Frank Lloyd Wright:
The Perspective
of a New Generation**

A symposium co-sponsored by
The Museum of Modern Art
and the Buell Center for the Study
of American Architecture

Friday, February 18, 7:00pm
at The Museum of Modern Art
Philip Johnson, Neil Levine

Saturday, February 19, 9:00am
at Columbia University
Wood Auditorium, Avery Hall
Terence Riley, Anthony Alofsin,
James O'Gorman, Kenneth Framp-
ton, Leo Marx, Alice T. Friedman,
Kathryn Smith

For further information
please call 854-8165

Building for Nature

The Architectural Landscapes
of Walter Burley Griffin
and Marion Lucy Mahony

January 31-February 26
100 Level
Avery Hall

Duneray

Spatial sequences generated
from a Cubist Painting:
computer drawings from
Duncan Brown

February 7-March 12
400 Level
Avery Hall

**Traces of
Islamic Architecture
in Spain**

Photographs by Anita Ayerbe

February 28-March 26
200 Level
Avery Hall

Luigi Snozzi

Buildings and projects
1958-1992

March 9-April 9
100 Level
Avery Hall

Student Projects

Current work

April 11-May 21
Buell Hall, Avery Hall

February

Colomina

Wednesday 16

Beatriz Colomina
Assistant Professor
of Architecture,
Princeton University
"Mies Not"

Wright

Saturday 19

Frank Lloyd Wright
"The Perspective
of a New Generation"
Symposium
(see details at right)

van Berkel

Wednesday 23

Ben van Berkel
Architect
Amsterdam, The Netherlands
"Crossing Points"

March

St.John Wilson

Wednesday 2

Colin St.John Wilson
Professor of Architecture,
Cambridge University,
"The Other Tradition"

Snozzi

Wednesday 9

Luigi Snozzi
Architect
Locarno, Switzerland
"Urban Projects"

Rogers

Thursday 10

Richard Rogers
Architect, London
"The Work of Richard
Rogers Partnership"

Seraji

Wednesday 23

Nasrine Seraji
Architect,
Paris and London
"The Event of Space"

Kipnis

Wednesday 30

Jeffrey Kipnis
Director of Graduate Design
Architectural Association
London
"The End of an -age"

April

Cook

Monday 18

Peter Cook
Bartlett Professor of
Architecture, The Bartlett
School of Architecture,
Building, Environmental
Design and Planning, London
"Instead of Greenery"

Design: Willi Kunz Associates, New York

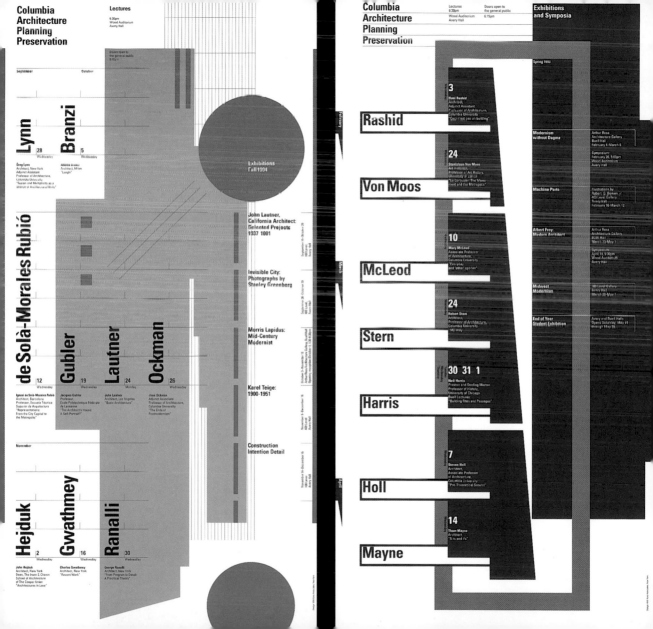

designer
Sloy

art director
Rudy VanderLans

design company
Emigre Graphics

country of origin
USA

work description
Advertising poster for
Emigre Graphics,
handlettered by Sloy

dimensions
830 x 570 mm
32⅝ x 22½ in

24

designer
Luca Dotti

college
Atelier Nationale de
Création Typographique,
Paris

country of origin
France

work description
Poster for Atelier
Nationale de Création
Typographique

dimensions
1700 x 596 mm
66⅞ x 23½ in

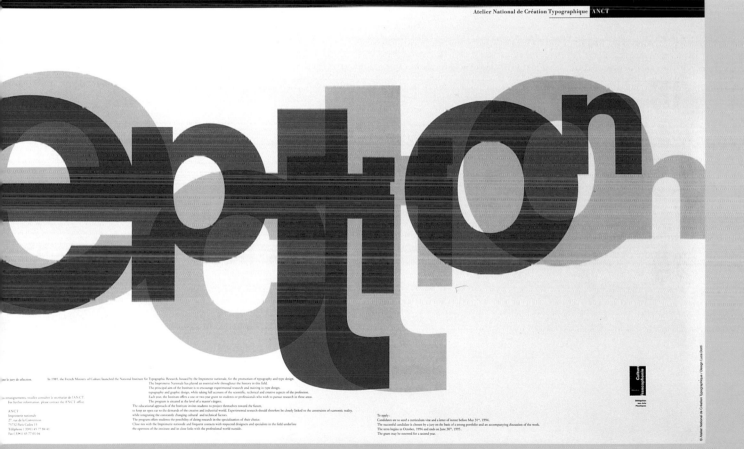

que le jury de sélection.

In 1985, the French Ministry of Culture launched the National Institute for Typographic Research, housed by the Imprimerie nationale, for the promotion of typography and type design.

The Imprimerie Nationale has played an essential role throughout the history in this field.

The principal aim of the Institute is to encourage experimental research and training in type design.

typography and graphic design, while taking full account of the scientific, technical and creative aspects of the profession.

Each year, the Institute offers a one or two year grant to students or professionals who wish to pursue research in these areas.

The program is situated at the level of a master's degree.

The educational approach of the Institute invites students to project themselves toward the future.

tra arrangements, veuillez consulter le secrétariat de l'ANCT.
For further information, please contact the ANCT office.

to keep an open ear to the demands of the creative and industrial world. Experimental research should therefore be closely linked to the constraints of economic reality.

while integrating the constantly changing cultural and technical factors.

The program offers students the possibility of doing research in the specialization of their choice.

Close ties with the Imprimerie nationale and frequent contacts with respected designers and specialists in the field underline

the openness of the institute and its close links with the professional world outside.

ANCT
Imprimerie nationale
27, rue de la Convention
75732 Paris Cedex 15
Téléphone : 33(1) 45 77 84 43
Fax : 33(1) 45 77 01 04

To apply:
Candidates are to send a curriculum vitæ and a letter of intent before May 31st, 1994.
The successful candidate is chosen by a jury on the basis of a strong portfolio and an accompanying discussion of the work.
The term begins in October, 1994 and ends on June 30th, 1995.
The grant may be renewed for a second year.

designer
The Designers Republic

country of origin
UK

work description
Dos Dedos Mis Amigos LP
by Pop Will Eat Itself
(Infectious Records, UK);
center of a gatefold
sleeve

dimensions
430 x 310 mm
16⅞ x 12¼ in

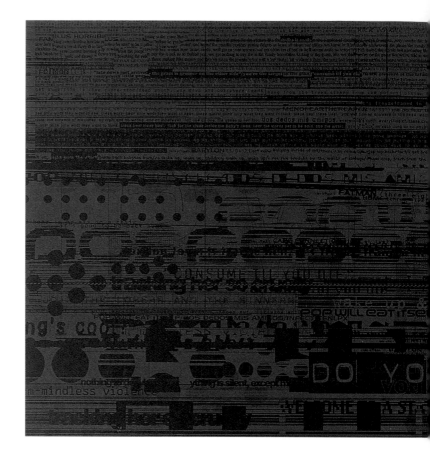

designer
The Designers Republic

country of origin
UK

work description
Aaah EP by Sun Electric,
(R & S records, Belgium);
center of a gatefold
sleeve

dimensions
430 x 310 mm
16⅞ x 12¼ in

designer
Caroline Pauchant

college
Ecole Nationale
Supérieure des Arts
Décoratifs, Paris

tutor
Philippe Apeloig

country of origin
France

work description
Qu'est ce que tu dis?, a
project based on a poem
by Raymond Queneau

dimensions
180 x 261 mm
7⅛ x 10¼ in

30

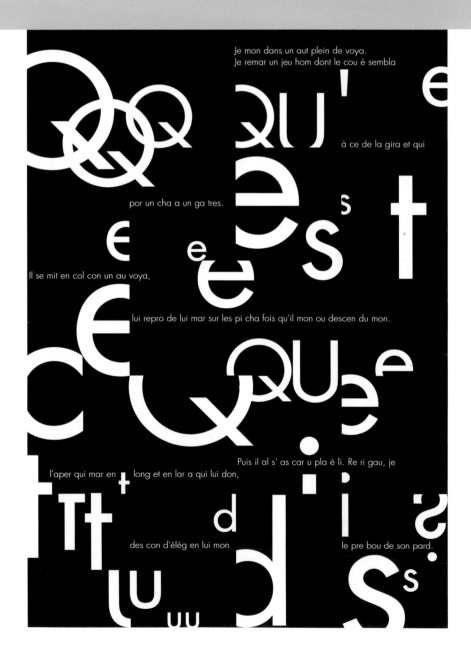

Déjeuner le matin
Il a mis le café
il a mis le lait
dans la tasse de café
il a mis le sucre
dans le café au lait
avec la petite cuillère
il l'a tourné
il a bu le café au lait

et il a reposé la tasse
sans me parler
il a allumé
une cigarette
il a fait des rondes
avec la fumée
Il a mis les cendres
dans le cendrier
sans me parler

sans me regarder
il s'est levé
il a mis son chapeau
sur la tête
il a mis son
manteau de pluie
parce qu'il pleuvait
et il est parti
sous la pluie

silence

sans une parole
sans me regarder
et moi j'ai pris ma
tête dans ma main
et j'ai pleuré.
Jacques Prévert

«qui parle avec moi?»

**Nous sommes
des muets
dans le monde
des muets.**

**Donc c'est à nous
de faire l'effort
d'apprendre leur
langage des signes
pour communiquer
avec eux.**

muets

designer
Anje Booken

college
École Nationale
Supérieure des Arts
Décoratifs, Paris

tutor
Philippe Apeloig

country of origin
France

work description
Muets/Silence, a project
based on a poem by
Jacques Prévert

dimensions
170 x 220 mm
6¾ x 8⅝ in

designer
Christophe Ambry

college
Ecole Nationale
Supérieure des Arts
Décoratifs, Paris

tutor
Philippe Apeloig

country of origin
France

work description
Project on Dyslexia

dimensions
200 x 303 mm
7⅞ x 11⅞ in

32

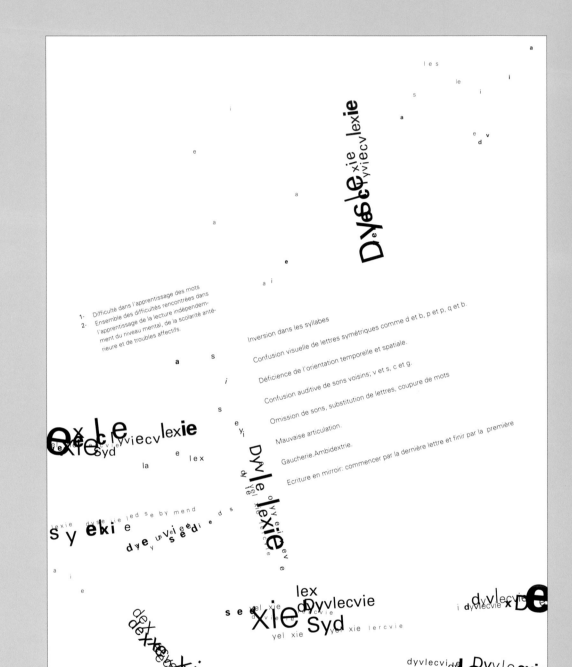

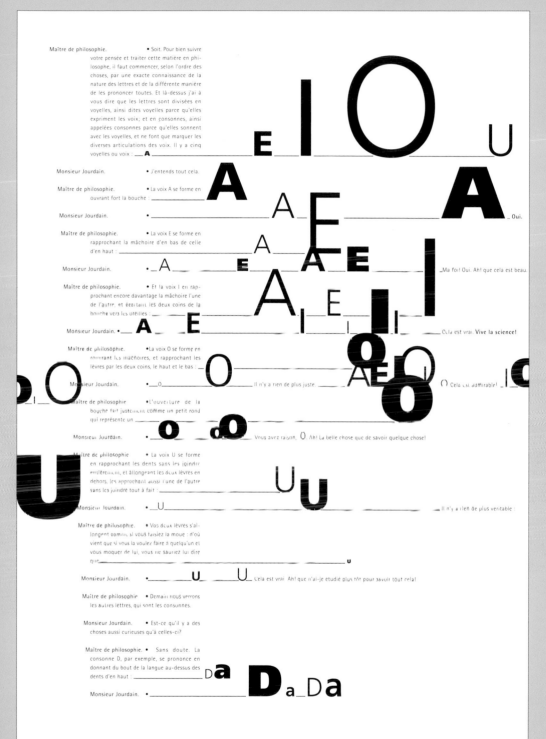

Maître de philosophie. • Soit. Pour bien suivre votre pensée et traiter cette matière en philosophe, il faut commencer, selon l'ordre des choses, par une exacte connaissance de la nature des lettres et de la différente manière de les prononcer toutes. Et là-dessus j'ai à vous dire que les lettres sont divisées en voyelles, ainsi dites voyelles parce qu'elles expriment les voix; et en consonnes, ainsi appelées consonnes parce qu'elles sonnent avec les voyelles, et ne font que marquer les diverses articulations des voix. Il y a cinq voyelles ou voix : A

Monsieur Jourdain. • J'entends tout cela.

Maître de philosophie. • La voix A se forme en ouvrant fort la bouche :

Monsieur Jourdain. • Oui.

Maître de philosophie. • La voix E se forme en rapprochant la mâchoire d'en bas de celle d'en haut :

Monsieur Jourdain. • Ma foi! Oui. Ah! que cela est beau.

Maître de philosophie. • Et la voix I en rapprochant encore davantage la mâchoire l'une de l'autre, et écartant les deux coins de la bouche vers les oreilles :

Monsieur Jourdain. • Cela est vrai. Vive la science!

Maître de philosophie. • La voix O se forme en rouvrant les mâchoires, et rapprochant les lèvres par les deux coins, le haut et le bas :

Monsieur Jourdain. • Il n'y a rien de plus juste. O Cela est admirable!

Maître de philosophie. • L'ouverture de la bouche fait justement comme un petit rond qui représente un O.

Monsieur Jourdain. • Vous avez raison, O. Ah! La belle chose que de savoir quelque chose!

Maître de philosophie. • La voix U se forme en rapprochant les dents sans les joindre entièrement, et allongeant les deux lèvres en dehors, les approchant aussi l'une de l'autre sans les joindre tout à fait :

Monsieur Jourdain. • U Il n'y a rien de plus véritable :

Maître de philosophie. • Vos deux lèvres s'allongent comme si vous faisiez la moue : d'où vient que si vous la voulez faire à quelqu'un et vous moquer de lui, vous ne sauriez lui dire que U.

Monsieur Jourdain. • U Cela est vrai! que n'ai-je étudié plus tôt pour savoir tout cela!

Maître de philosophie. • Demain nous verrons les autres lettres, qui sont les consonnes.

Monsieur Jourdain. • Est-ce qu'il y a des choses aussi curieuses qu'à celles-ci?

Maître de philosophie. • Sans doute. La consonne D, par exemple, se prononce en donnant du bout de la langue au-dessus des dents d'en haut : Da Da

Monsieur Jourdain. • Da Da

designer
Jérôme Mouscadet

college
Ecole Nationale
Supérieure des Arts
Décoratifs, Paris

tutor
Philippe Apeloig

country of origin
France

work description
AEIOU, a project based
on *Le Bourgeois
Gentilhomme*, a play
by Molière

dimensions
244 x 360 mm
9⅝ x 14⅛ in

33

designer
Dirk van Dooren

design company
Tomato

country of origin
UK

work description
Detail from a poster
for the Institute of
Contemporary Art,
London

dimensions
550 x 510 mm
21 ⅝ x 20 in

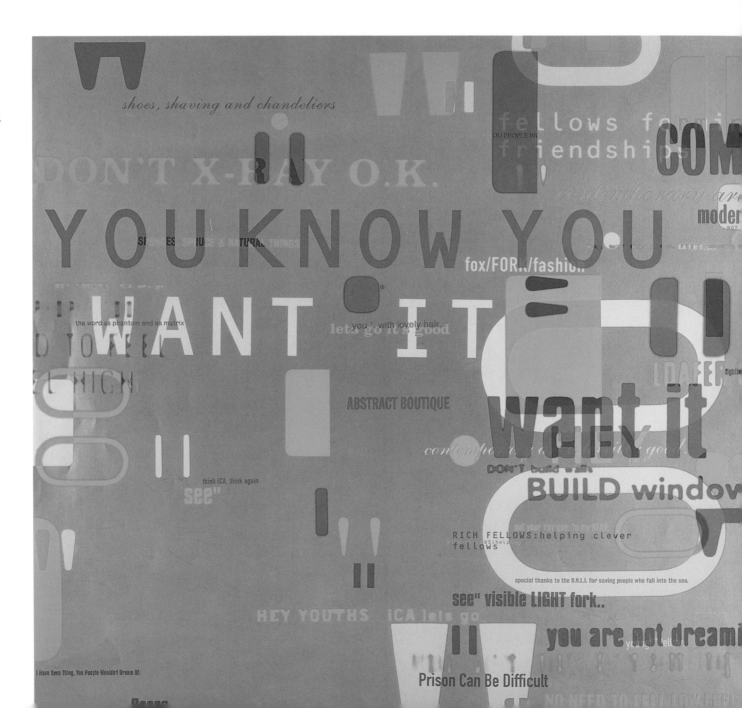

designers
Lies Ros
Rob Schröder

design company
Wild Plakken

country of origin
The Netherlands

work description
The last poster of the
Dutch Anti-Apartheid
Movement, announcing
an event to celebrate the
end of apartheid in South
Africa: BLANK (white)
and BLACK (black)
cooperating

dimensions
594 x 840 mm
23⅜ x 33 in

designer
Melle Hammer

design company
Plus X

country of origin
The Netherlands

work description
Het Ontbrekend Teken [*The Missing Sign*], a poster

dimensions
605 x 280 mm
23¾ x 11 in

zaterdag 10 december
aanvang: 20.00 u.
Stichting Perdu,
Kerkstraat 591
Toegang ƒ 7.50
Tel. 6234874
'Het ontbreken
door de vakklas
typografie van d
Gerrit Rietveld A
samen met Stichting Perdu en
veertien auteurs

designer
Karen Wilks

design company
Karen Wilks Associates

country of origin
UK

work description
One from a set of four
self-promotional
postcards for 1994

dimensions
105 x 148 mm
4⅛ x 5⅞ in

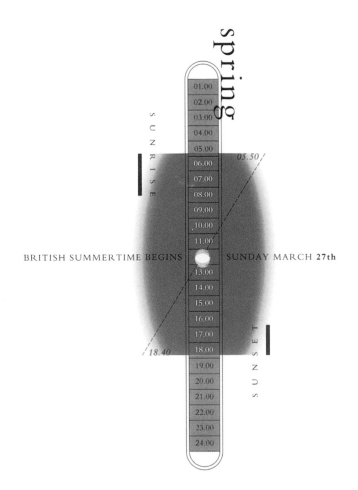

designer
Karen Wilks

design company
Karen Wilks Associates

country of origin
UK

work description
One from a set of four
self-promotional
postcards for 1995

dimensions
148 x 105 mm
5⅞ x 4⅛ in

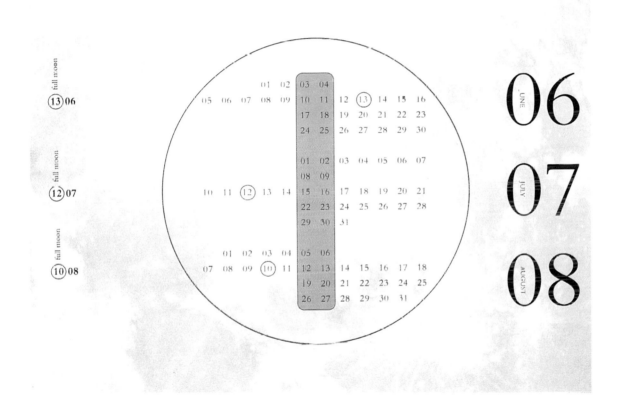

designer
Huw Morgan

country of origin
UK

work description
Idiot Boy, a project for
the Royal College of Art,
London, that explores
attitudes toward the
mentally ill

dimensions
1524 x 1016 mm
60 x 40 in

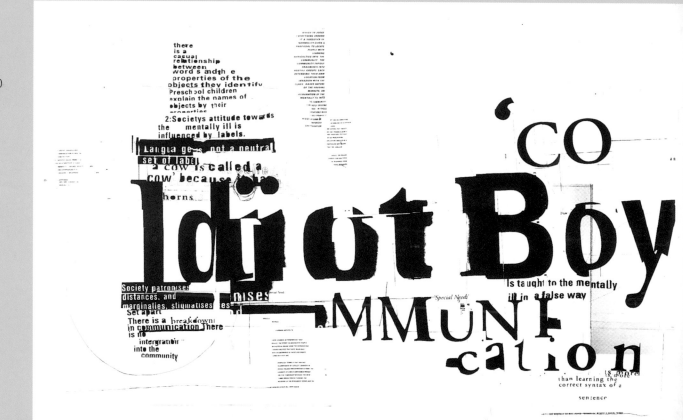

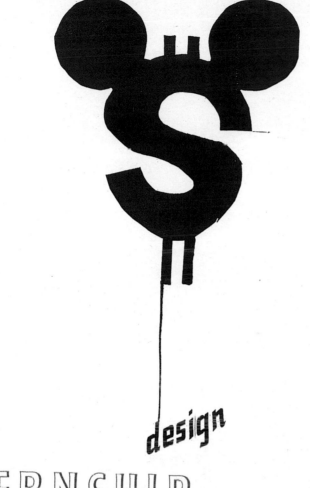

design

INTERNSHIP

$400—500 weekly

The Disney Store, Inc.

SUBMIT RESUME AND COVER LETTER TO STUDENT AFFAIRS

SEE WILHEMINE SCHAEFFER FOR DETAILS

designers
Michael Worthington
Christa Skinner

college
California Institute of
the Arts

country of origin
USA

work description
*Internship: The Disney
Store Inc,* a poster

dimensions
200 x 431 mm
11 x 17 in

designers
Betina Muller
Birgit Tummers
Claudia Trauer
Nauka Kirschner
Petra Reisdorf

design company
Atelier

country of origin
Germany

work description
Berliner Sommernacht der Lyrik, third in a series of posters for the annual summernight of lyric poetry, read in the garden of the Berlin Literaturwerkstatt [literature workshop]

dimensions
840 x 594 mm
33⅛ x 23⅜ in

designer
Jim Ross

design company
Mirelez/Ross Inc.

country of origin
USA

work description
Clayfest No. 8, an
exhibition poster

dimensions
660 x 874 mm
25⅞ x 34⅜ in

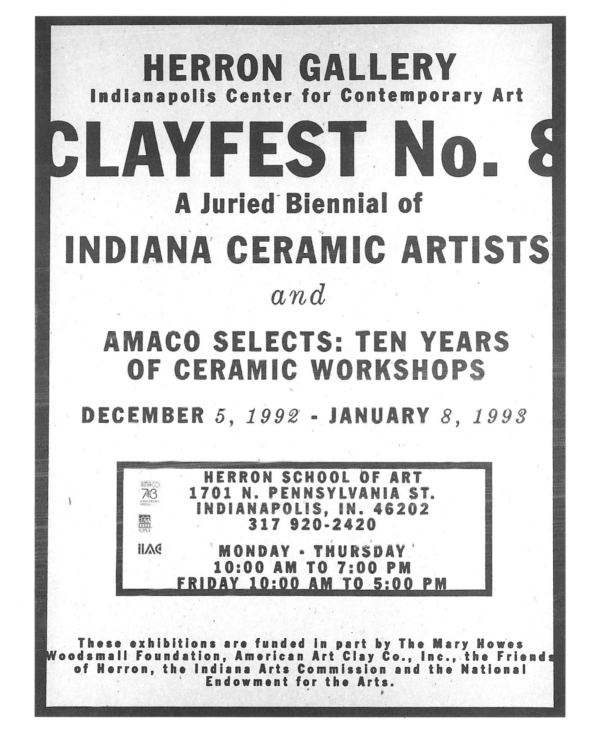

designers
Karl Hyde
John Warwicker

design company
Tomato

country of origin
UK

work description
Spreads and details from
the book *Skyscraper*, for
Booth-Clibborn publishers

dimensions
205 x 297 mm
8⅛ x 11¾ in

designers
Fernando Gutiérrez
Pablo Martín

photographer
Marie Espeus

art director
Fernando Gutiérrez

design company
Martín & Gutiérrez

country of origin
Spain

work description
Front cover, cover verso,
title, and opening page of
text from an exhibition
catalog

dimensions
165 x 295 mm
6½ x 11⅝ in

ÉCARTS

PERET

SEPTEMBRE NOVEMBRE 1994

LE MONDE DE L'ART

PARIS

Dans

la hiérarchie des accep-
tions du mot écart que l'on trouve dans Le Petit Robert celui qui s'en identifie le plus est celle définie en numéro 6. On y lit : "Loc. adv. À L'ÉCART dans un
endroit écarté, à une certaine distance (de la foule, d'un groupe). Vivre…, etc."
Et pour préciser encore plus, c'est avec le sens, à une certaine distance que je
m'identifie. Pointilleux je le suis, je tiens à signaler que ce n'est pas à distance
de la foule ou d'un groupe que je veux me placer, au contraire c'est plutôt à une
certaine distance de moi-même que je cherche à me tenir jusqu'à présent j'ai
travaillé dans le graphisme et l'illustration. J'ai pu jouer avec toute sorte de
moyens d'expression. J'ai touché à tout, ou presque, dans le domaine de la
communication. Mais on n'exerce pas impunément un métier pendant vingt
cinq années sans s'en lasser. C'est dans un sous par rapport à une route pro-
fessionnelle, qui même variée, est trop balisée et n'arrive plus à combler les ca-
prices de ma curiosité. Le seul moyen pour moi, il y est d'aller c'était de suivre
une impulsion, de travailler sur une intuition.

Malheureusement cela n'a pas été facile. Car ce n'est qu'avec une perspective
différente que l'on peut essayer de se comprendre, de sortir l'ensemble. Se voir
du dehors pour essayer de décortiquer ce qu'on est et ce qu'on fait, bien qu'être
et faire soient indivisiblement liés.

Tout d'abord pas l'effet de miroir, par l'un de mieux que l'on même pour avoir une
approche de soi-même. Un de mes amis soutient que l'on est obligé de cultiver
les symboles dans lesquels on se reconnaît et que nous constituent, que c'est
dans la qualité des miroirs, dans lesquels on cherche notre reflet, que l'on peut
recouvrer notre fragile identité et mesurer notre taille. Je ne saurais être plus en
accord. Les miroirs dans lesquels je suis et me cherche ont été variés mais
reliés par le fil invisible des attitudes. Je suis en tout, aujourd'hui, des reconnais-
sant à ces miroirs, car ils ne m'ont pas souvent renvoyé mon image, ils me
l'ont rendue enrichie de tous leurs trésors et en plus ils m'ont appris à regarder.
À regarder, à voir et à apprécier la richesse cachée dans le plus humble des
objets. ...

designer
Alan Kitching

illustrator
Raffaella Fletcher

design company
The Typography Workshop

art director
Alan Kitching

country of origin
UK

work description
Posters and the slip-case
(overlaid, right) from *A
Brief History of Type* (self-
published)

dimensions
slip-case
210 x 210 mm
8¼ x 8¼ in

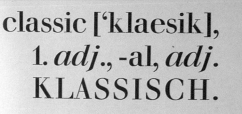

classic ['klaesik],
1. *adj.*, -al, *adj.*
KLASSISCH.

Justus Erich Walbaum of Weimar   1800

INFERNO

AmerikAtla

DANTE L'

ntiCable. 1927

designer
Anukam Edward Opara

college
London College of
Printing and Distributive
Trades

country of origin
UK

work description
HET, a page from a
calendar of typographers
and designers: Julius
[June] represents the
Hungarian designer,
Moholy-Nagy, with the
typeface Akzindenz
Grotesk Regular

dimensions
1680 x 2376 mm
66⅛ x 93½ in

50

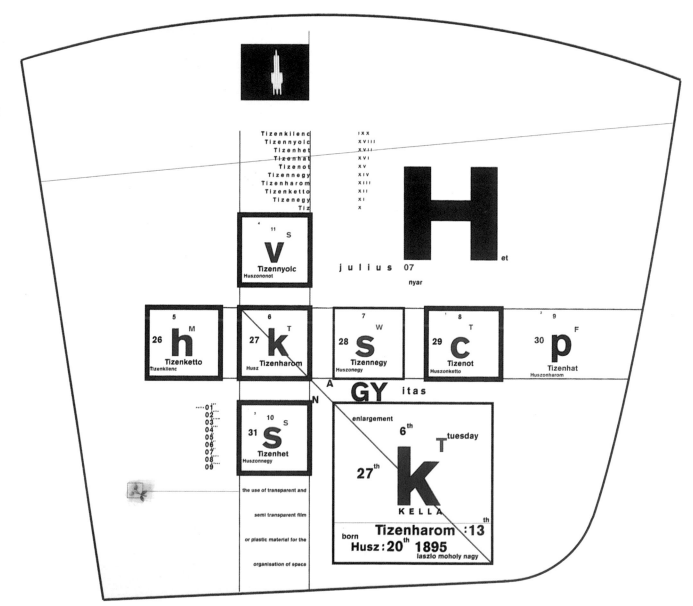

designer
David Harlan

college
California Institute of
the Arts

country of origin
USA

work description
Sketch for an information
system

dimensions
279 x 216 mm
11 x 8½ in

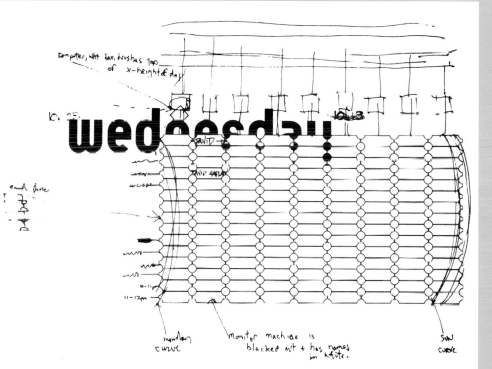

designer
Chris Roberts

college
Bath College of Higher
Education

country of origin
UK

work description
Front and back of a
double-sided degree show
poster, on tracing paper,
for Bath College

dimensions
594 x 420 mm
23⅜ x 16½ in

designer
Chris Roberts

college
Bath College of Higher Education

country of origin
UK

work description
Lecture poster

dimensions
600 x 450 mm
23⅝ x 17¾ in

designer
Jörg Herzog

art director
Jörg Herzog

design company
Herzog Grafik und Design

country of origin
Germany

work description
Pages from a calendar

dimensions
420 x 594 mm
16½ x 23⅜ in

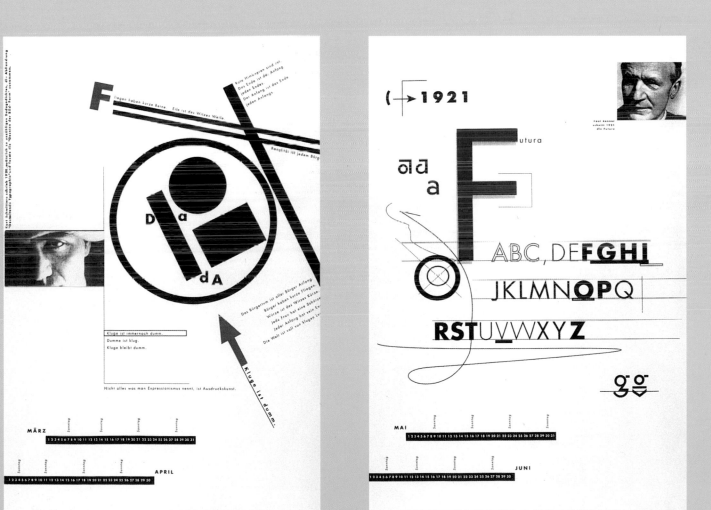

left and below

designer
Hans P. Brandt

design company
Total Design

country of origin
The Netherlands

work description
Front cover and spread
from the 1993 Annual
Report for Internationales
Design Zentrum, Berlin

dimensions
210 x 297 mm
8¼ x 11¾ in

56

right

designers
Weston Bingham
Chuck Rudy

design company
Deluxe

country of origin
USA

work description
Stationery for Deluxe
design company

dimensions
letterhead
215 x 280 mm
8½ x 11 in

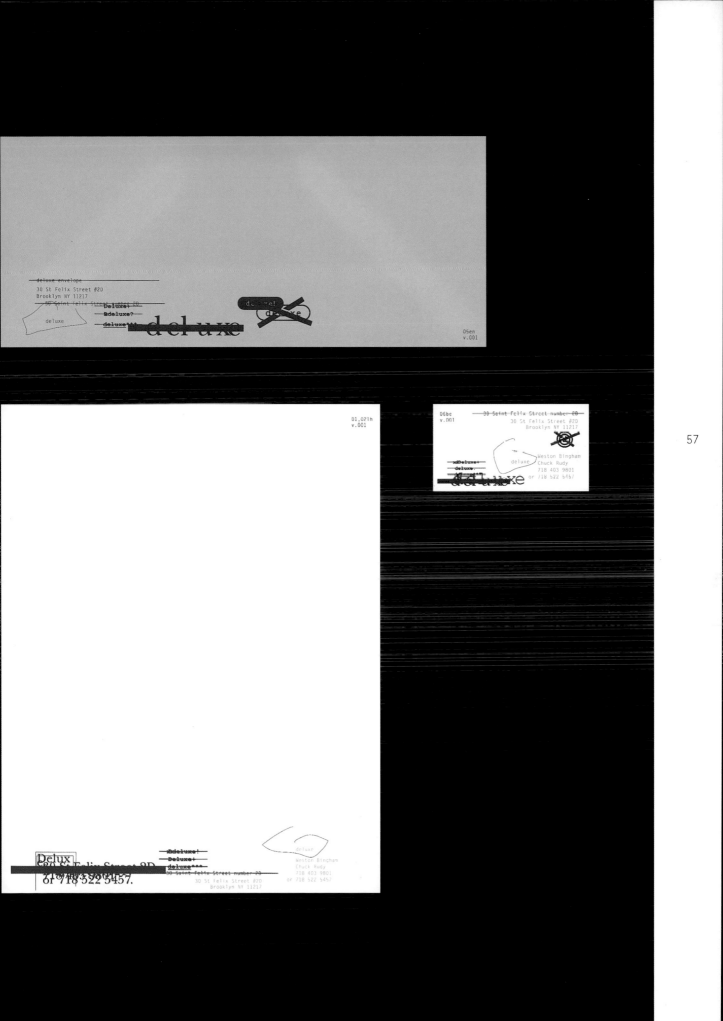

deluxe envelope
30 St Felix Street #2D
Brooklyn NY 11217
30 Saint Felix Street number 2D
Deluxe!
Bdeluxe?
deluxe
deluxe***
deluxe

deluxe!
deluxe

01.02lh
v.001

05en
v.001

06be
v.001
30 Saint Felix Street number 2D
30 St Felix Street #2D
Brooklyn NY 11217

adDeluxe!
deluxe.
deluxe
deluxe   Weston Bingham
Chuck Rudy
718 403 9801
or 718 522 5457

deluxe
Weston Bingham
Chuck Rudy
718 403 9801
or 718 522 5457

Delux
30 St Felix Street 2D
or 718 522 5457.
Bdeluxe!
Deluxe!
deluxe***
30 Saint Felix Street number 2D
30 St Felix Street #2D
Brooklyn NY 11217

designer
Neil Fletcher

design company
Pd-p

country of origin
UK

work description
Peaches and Cream, a
poster for Sheffield
Hallam University Union
of Students

dimensions
594 x 840 mm
5½ x 7⅛ in

designers
Elisabeth Charman
Edwin Utermohlen

art directors
Elisabeth Charman
Edwin Utermohlen

design company
doubledagger

country of origin
USA

work description
Poster for the Herron
Gallery (unpublished)

dimensions
250 x 320 mm
9⁷/₈ x 12⁵/₈ in

Herron Gallery

Indianapolis Center for Contemporary Art

Herron School of Art

1701 North Pennsylvania Street, Indianapolis, Indiana 46202
telephone # 317.920.2420

Monday—Thursday 10:00am–7:00pm
Friday 10:00am–5:00pm

IUPUI

FACULTY SHOW
(Part 2)
DATES: FEBRUARY 3—MARCH 10
1995

STUDENT SHOW[S]
MARCH 17—APRIL 7 + APRIL 14—MAY 5, 1995

designers
Laura Lacy-Sholly
James Sholly

design company
Antenna

country of origin
USA

work description
Front cover and spreads
from the *Indiana Civil
Liberties Datebook*, an
educational tool for the
Indiana Civil Liberties
Union with the theme
"Who Decides?"

dimensions
140 x 180 mm
5½ x 7⅛ in

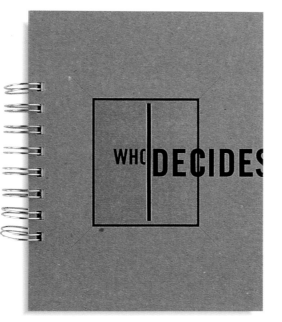

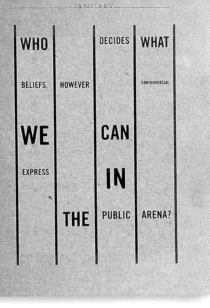

WHO **DECIDES** **WHAT**

BELIEFS, HOWEVER CONTROVERSIAL

WE **CAN**

EXPRESS **IN**

THE **PUBLIC** **ARENA?**

There's something inspiring about a new calendar:
365 blank spaces, all of them awaiting your plans,
aspirations and activities. . .

the promise of a fresh year and the chance to spend time more wisely.

(Or at least to try.)

I think there's something *awe-inspiring* about this new calendar. While it certainly will tell you what date to write at the top of your checks, the 1995 I.C.L.U. Datebook is so much more. It's a repository of wise words. It's a gathering of friends. It's a hard-working fundraiser. Most of all, it's a labor of love.

We're thrilled that you've chosen to make this book a part of your new year. We hope that you'll take the time to explore all that it holds. Notice the many bits of wisdom out on each week, from the creative

thinkers and civil libertarians of the last few centuries. Deep in February, when you cannot else to one more stark, gray day, just open your datebook. Oscar Wilde's commentary on truth will give you a jump-start.

Your new calendar brings together friends from around the state. Hoosiers of all ages and persuasions have given both the time and financial resources to make this project possible. Many have teamed up with colleagues to underwrite particular dates. Others have worked on producing the book. Still others apply themselves behind the scenes presenting and promoting the ideas represented in these pages.

M

Who decides the value of the maternal link?

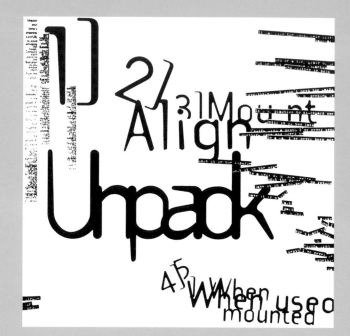

designer
Shelley Stepp

college
California Institute of
the Arts

country of origin
USA

work description
Typographic assignments
based on poetic and
didactic texts

dimensions
254 x 254 mm
10 x 10 in

62

designer
Shelley Stepp

college
California Institute of
the Arts

country of origin
USA

work description
Studies with identical
texts – the changing
forms create new
meanings

dimensions
762 x 762 mm
30 x 30 in

designer
Jan C. Almquist

art directors
Jan C. Almquist
Hans-U. Allemann

design company
Allemann Almquist &
Jones

country of origin
USA

work description
Front cover of
A Compelling Argument,
a brochure for the
Winchell Company,
printers

dimensions
158 x 292 mm
6¼ x 11½ in

A Compelling

A

Argument

From concept to result

designers
Stephen Shackleford
Jan C. Almquist

art directors
Jan C. Almquist
Hans-U. Allemann

design company
Allemann Almquist &
Jones

country of origin
USA

work description
Front cover of *From
Concept to Result*, a
brochure for the Winchell
Company, printers

dimensions
158 x 292 mm
6¼ x 11½ in

65

designer
Christopher Ashworth

design company
Invisible

country of origin
UK

work description
Letterhead for Shaun
Bloodworth; designed for
a typewriter with a wide
carriage

dimensions
297 x 210 mm
11¾ x 8¼ in

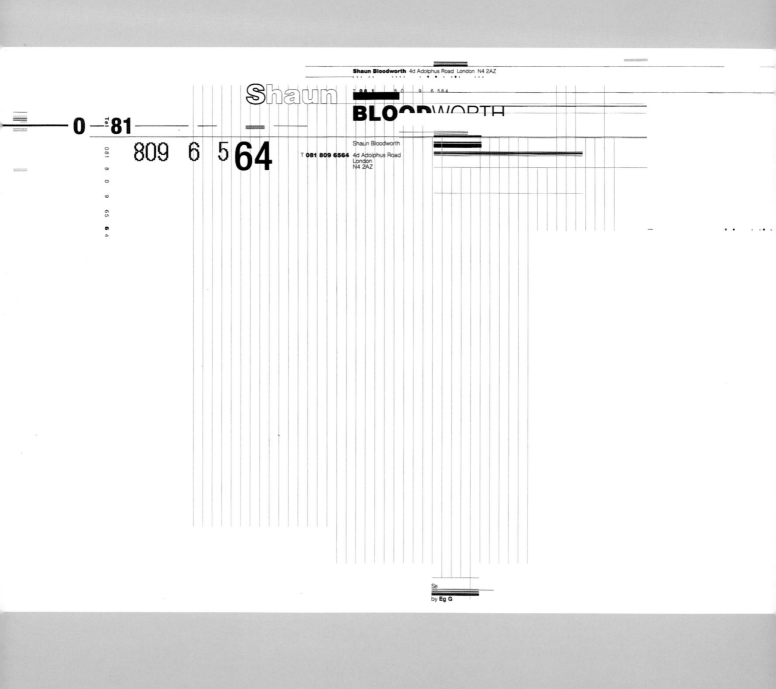

designer
Jeremy Francis Mende

work description
Dada Invoice

college
Cranbrook Academy of
Art, Michigan

dimensions
203 x 254 mm
8 x 10 in

country of origin
USA

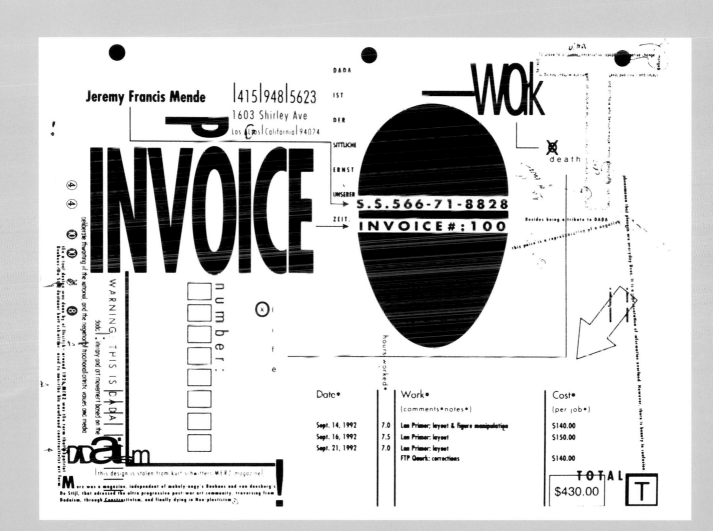

designer
Christopher Ashworth

design company
Orange

art director
Christopher Ashworth

country of origin
UK

work description
Three flyers from a set of
four, for Libido Nightclub

dimensions
right and far right
206 x 99 mm
8⅛ x 3⅞ in
far right, below
130 x 130 mm
5⅛ x 5⅛ in

LIBIDO

a new night for sheffield
every friday at occasions
town centre
starting date 31 July

Price: £5 every week Deano - Sheffield Gary Norman - Leeds Sully - Sheffield   plus

Fabi Paris 31 July
C J Mackintosh 7 August
Dave Seaman 14 August
Jon Da Silva 21 August

designer
John O'Callaghan

college
Ravensbourne College
of Design and
Communication,
Chislehurst

tutor
Paul Elliman

country of origin
UK

work description
Spreads from a project
responding to media
representation of the
Gulf War

dimensions
420 x 594 mm
16½ x 23⅜ in

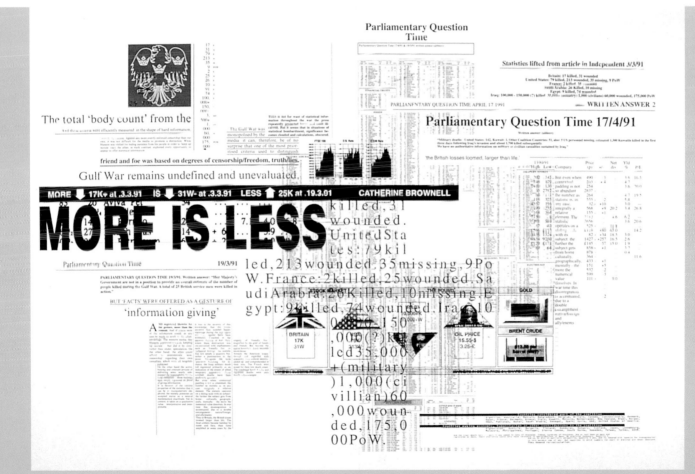

type plus

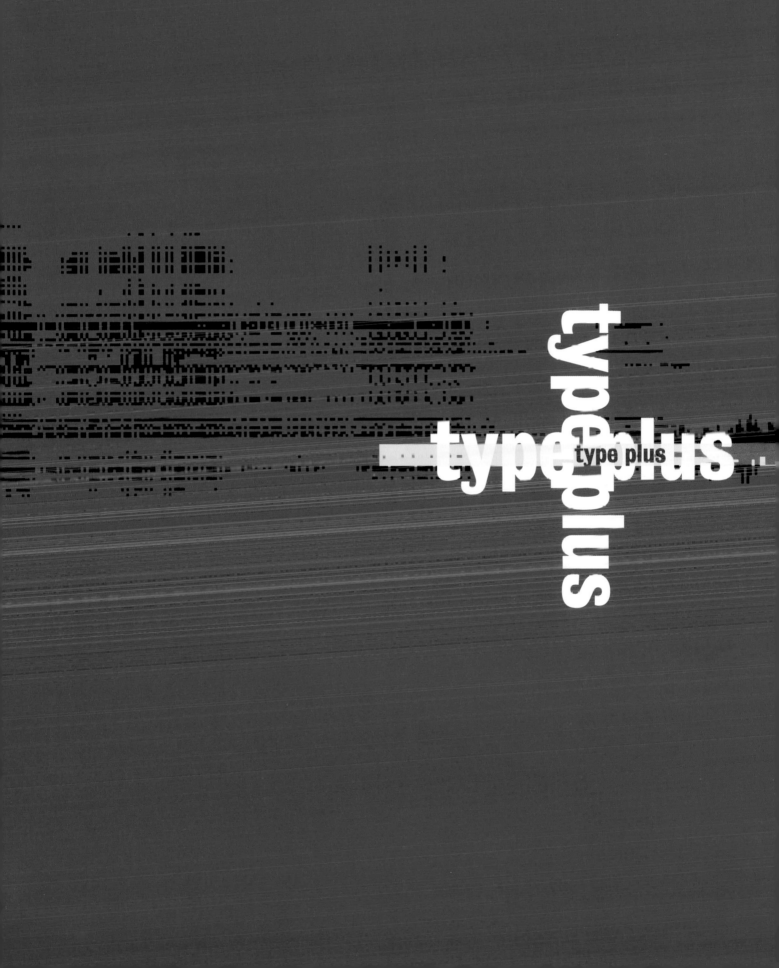

designers
Simon Taylor
Dirk van Dooren

design company
Tomato

country of origin
UK

work description
Promotional photographs
for Urban Reaction
Clothing Label, Japan

dimensions
51 x 76 mm
2 x 3 in

left

designer
The Designers Republic

country of origin
UK

work description
The Designers Republic
vs the Entire Population
of Sweden, a self-
promotional poster

dimensions
297 x 420 mm
11¾ x 16½ in

right

designer
Dirk van Dooren

art director
Trichett & Webb

design company
Tomato

country of origin
UK

work description
Page from a self-promotional
calendar

dimensions
325 x 410 mm
12¾ x 16⅛ in

designers
Heather Ferguson
Amy Jo Banton

photographers
Heather Ferguson
Amy Jo Banton

art directors
Heather Ferguson
Amy Jo Banton

78

design company
2 Bellybuttons

country of origin
USA

work description
Front cover and spread
from the magazine *Flying
the Coupe*

dimensions
253 x 305 mm
10 x 12 in

H: how were the mounds discovered? I mean how did they discover the mounds? W: the mounds here? H: yeah W: they're pretty evident H: they are? W: you got one out there that's 70, over 70 feet high H: wow W: so i mean you're gonna stumble over them H: yeah AJ: (laughter) W: the mounds have been known, they were first reported in the 1860's, 1870's H: uh-huhh W: like the ridges were not discovered until the 1950's, when this aireal view photograph was found H: oh W: here were some people working there, they knew they had a huge site H: yeah W: but, ahh, they were digging on mound B over that, that a way. and, ahhh, James Ford from the American Museum of Natural History went over to Vicksburg Waterways experimental station and he got and he found this photograph, WE RIDGES!! and you can see them. Actually this earlier photograph shows them but no one ever noticed H: they just didn't odd that there was another indian hill and um, there you are (AJ has finally located subject with view camera) H subdivision around it W: okay, north of Monroe? AJ & H: yeah W: yeah, that's Frenchman's Bend and, ah, that was W: and, ah, it was very exciting and they're not destroying it, they're just kind of working around it and they're gonna have mounds will be part of the golf course AJ: oh really W: uh huh W: wow H: (laughter) W: yeah the developer there has been very, very responsible and it's really great to have some one like that AJ: yeah, we saw it, we saw it yesterday. it was, it just seems really strange. usually they, you know, usually, like in Virginia they would just, like, put up, ah, you know, i don't know, sort of like a place. they would put up a whole monument around it and everything W: well we have too many of them AJ: oh really W: yeah if you were to do that with every indian site, you would have problems AJ: yeah W: and, ah, further more, the state doesn't have the money to do it, so... AJ: so why don't they just excavate them and... W: all right what happens when you excavate a site? AJ: everybody gets all up in a uproar. i don't know about moving the artifacts W: no, stop and think when you've excavated a site, what happens to that site? H: it's been destroyed W: so therefore, the best thing to do on a site is to excavate enough to find out what you need know and then leave, because techniques change H: yeah W: ah, i went on my first dig in 1955 H: wow W: an the differences in the way digs are done then and now are just incalcuable H: uh huh W: the different techniques and everything else from what we've been able to find H: yeah W: ah, see i was digging in the southwest about the time they were finding that photograph H: wow W: and ah, so as a result, no you don't want to dig them H: you destroy them W: no you want to preserve them by putting a golf course on it it's perfectly preserved H: yeah W: what's going to happen? you're going to mow the grass. H: (laughter) AJ: yeah but don't you think all these unknowns will try to excavate themselves? W: no AJ: you don't think so? H: (laughter) W: because all the local pot hunters know that there's nothing in there worth it H: yeah W: i mean it's that site okay, the type of material that's in that site is microflint, they found one or two points and they found lots of fire-cracked rock which is really something H: yeah AJ & H: (laughter) W: it's nothing to write home to mother about, so that's

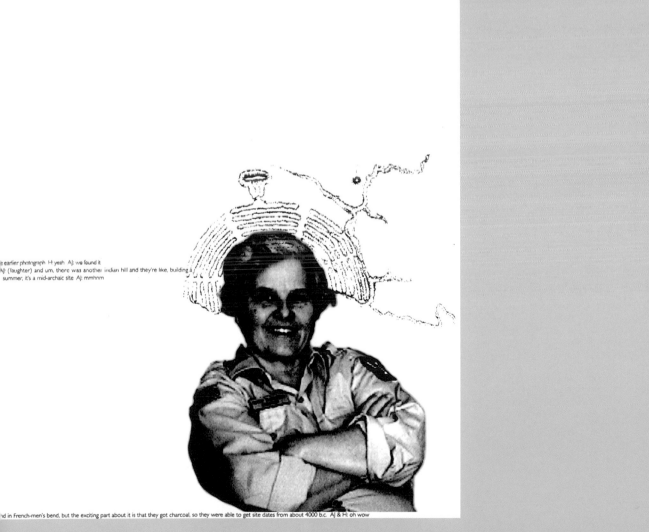

earlier photograph H: yeah AJ: we found it

AJ: (laughter) and um, there was another indian hill and they're like, building

summer, it's a mid-archaic site AJ: mmhnm

nd in French-men's bend, but the exciting part about it is that they got charcoal, so they were able to get site dates from about 4000 b.c. AJ & H: oh wow

below

designers
Paula Benson
Paul West

photographer
Spiros

art directors
Paula Benson
Paul West

design company
Form

country of origin
UK

work description
Spread from a press
release in the form of a
mini newspaper, for 2WO
THIRD3

dimensions
294 x 415 mm
11⅝ x 16⅜ in

right

designers
Paula Benson
Paul West

photographers
above
Lawrence Watson
below
Tim Platt

art directors
Paula Benson
Paul West

design company
Form

country of origin
UK

work description
I Want the World and *Ease
the Pressure*, open CD
boxes for 2WO THIRD3

dimensions
140 x 125 mm
5½ x 5 in

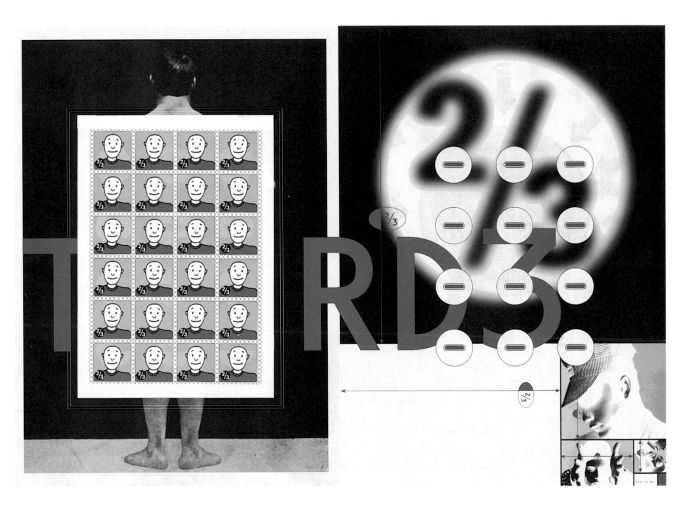

Columbia University
Graduate School of Architecture
Planning and Preservation

Introduction to Architecture

A Summer Studio in New York

designer
Willi Kunz

photographers
right
Skyviews
far right
Richard Plunz

design company
Willi Kunz Associates

82 **country of origin**
USA

work description
Program posters for
Columbia University,
Graduate School of
Architecture, Planning,
and Preservation, New
York

dimensions
305 x 609 mm
12 x 24 in

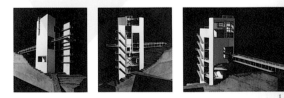

A summer program giving university credit which introduces the student to aspects of the design, history, theory, and practice of architecture. The program is intended both for those without previous academic experience in design who are interested in architecture as a potential career, and for those with previous experience in architectural design who would like to develop additional studio design skills, perhaps in preparation for application to graduate school.

Courses are given in the studios of Avery Hall, home of Columbia University's world-renowned Graduate School of Architecture, Planning, and Preservation, on the Morningside Heights campus in New York City. Studios and seminar courses are taught by experienced architects and designers, coordinated and supervised by members of the faculty of the Graduate School. For those who may require it, housing is available on the University campus, with direct access to Avery Hall.

Students attend classes four days a week for five weeks, both morning and afternoon sessions. In the morning session, students are introduced to the fundamentals of architectural history and theory, structures, technology, and professional practice. Also, this course will introduce the student to the extraordinary city of New York, with its world famous collection of museums, cultural institutions, and architectural monuments. Lectures, seminar presentations, tours of architect's offices, and field-trips to active building sites, museums, and famous works of architecture in New York City are led by the instructors.

In addition, students will attend a series of special lectures to be given by distinguished and renowned architects, including the following:

Kenneth Frampton
Architect; professor; author of "Modern Architecture: A Critical History"

Steven Holl
Architect; professor; winner of numerous Progressive Architecture Awards

James Stewart Polshek
Architect; professor; designer for the renovation of Carnegie Hall

Robert A. M. Stern
Architect; professor; author of "Pride of Place"

Bernard Tschumi
Architect; Dean, Columbia University; designer of the park "La Villette", Paris

In the afternoon, the students attend the design studio – an educational method unique to architecture – a place where students are given an intensive training in the skills and critical thinking involved in architectural design. Students, in small groups, work directly with studio instructors to develop their individual designs, which the students then present in periodic reviews or "juries", where they hear the comments and criticism of the invited architects and professors. The design projects given in studio are frequently situated in New York City, so that the student is able to apply the knowledge he or she has gained from the morning sessions. The development of supporting skills such as drawing and model building is also included in the studio curriculum.

Together the studio and lectures present a comprehensive introduction to every aspect of architecture as it is practiced today. In addition, through the various field-trips and tours, the student learns from the extraordinary examples of architectural and urban design in New York City, the world's preeminent center for architectural culture.

Program Director:
Thomas Hanrahan,
Architect; professor

Introduction to Architecture:
July 6 to August 8
Monday, Tuesday, Wednesday, Thursday
10:00am–5:00pm
3 credits, studio and seminar
Tuition for 1992: $1590
Housing on the Columbia University campus (if required): approximately $600

Applications should include a transcript of the applicant's academic record; a resume summarizing education, employment, and other types of experience; and, where appropriate, examples of the applicant's design work. Also please include a $35 application fee (checks made out to: Columbia University).

Applications are due by June 30

For information and
applications write or call:

Office of Admissions –
Introduction to
Architecture Program
Columbia University
Graduate School
of Architecture, Planning,
and Preservation
400 Avery Hall
New York, NY 10027
(212) 854-3414

Master of Science in Architecture and Urban Design

The Master of Science Degree in Architecture and Urban Design is an intensive three semester program for architects interested in post-professional design specialization.

Program

The curriculum is oriented toward the emerging urbanism in the United States, with a particular emphasis on the situation in New York City. It seeks to define parameters and problems which will carry into the next century. It also embraces a special relationship between the design studio and New York, through collaboration with city agencies and other public interest constituencies. Comparative study with other world cities is also considered central to the pedagogic structure, focused on seminars and case studies.

Emphasis

The degree is intended to augment traditional professional training in architecture for those who wish to further investigate the physical aspects of urbanism. "Urban Design" is seen as an activist, social art more than a singular representation of physical scale, the term defines a commitment to discourse at all scales of design activity. The design studio is the primary catalyst for the curriculum, centered on a highly individualized, atelier approach. The unique situation of Columbia allows New York City to become a laboratory, in which the discipline of architecture can be applied to a myriad of problems within our urban environment at all scales of inquiry. At the same time, the more theoretical component of coursework allows for comparative study with other world cities and situations. The final studio affords an opportunity for comparative study between New York and another world city.

Resources

The Columbia University Graduate School of Architecture, Planning and Preservation is a unique academic forum within which to pursue studies in Urban Design. The distinguished, multidisciplinary faculty nurtures a wide ranging critical perspective on the question of urbanism today. Classroom and studio teaching is reinforced by extensive lecture and publication programs. The Avery Architectural and Fine Arts Library is an invaluable resource, as the nation's finest repository for the literature of architecture, planning, and fine arts. In addition, the innumerable cultural resources of New York City, as a whole, are close at hand.

Bernard Tschumi, Dean
Richard Plunz, Director

Further information and application:
Columbia University
Office of Architecture Admissions
400 Avery Hall
New York, NY 10027
212 854 3414

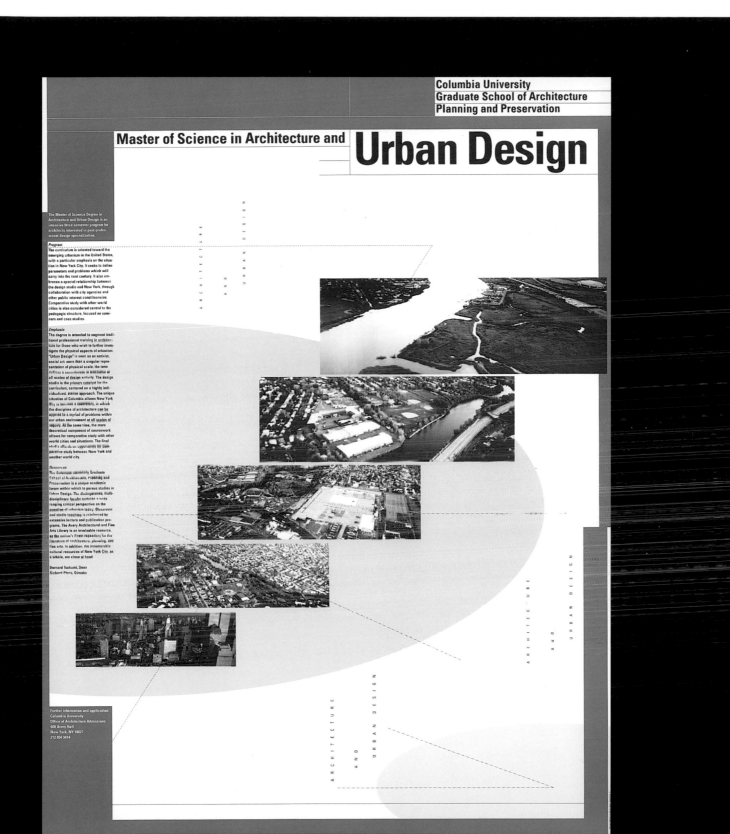

designer
David de Jong

photographers
Jurjen de Jong
David de Jong

college
Utrecht School of
the Arts

country of origin
The Netherlands

work description
Box lid (below, left), open
box (below, right) and
spreads (far right) from
An Interactive Book; texts
are linked by symbols and
numbers which allow the
book to be read in several
directions (unpublished)

dimensions
box size
345 x 345 mm
13⅝ x 13⅝ in

84

What is painting?
Well, it is literature.
What is literature then?
Well, it is painting.
What is the rest?
The rest is demotion.
Like the moon when she is full,
When she is a slender crescent,
When she is black theoretical night.

designers
Carlo Tartaglia
Robert Lamb

college
Ravensbourne College
of Design and
Communication,
Chislehurst

tutor
Rupert Bassett

country of origin
UK

work description
Cover and spreads from
the 1993 Ravensbourne
College degree show
publication

dimensions
297 x 420 mm
11¾ x 16½ in

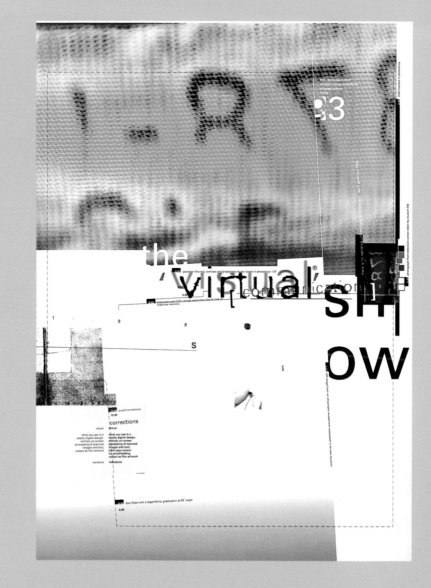

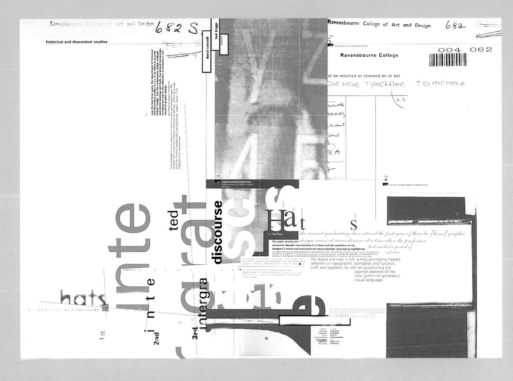

designer
The Designers Republic

country of origin
UK

work description
Tournesol by Kokotsu, LP
(R & S Records, Belgium);
center of gatefold sleeve

dimensions
430 x 310 mm
16⅞ x 12¼ in

designer
The Designers Republic

photographers
Phil Wolstenholme
Jess Scott-Hunter
David Slade

country of origin
UK

work description
Artificial Intelligence II,
compilation LP (Warp
Records, UK); center of
gatefold sleeve

dimensions
430 x 310 mm
16⅞ x 12¼ in

designer
Iain Cadby

country of origin
UK

work description
Two self-published
posters, from a set of
three

dimensions
210 x 297 mm
8¼ x 11¾ in

90

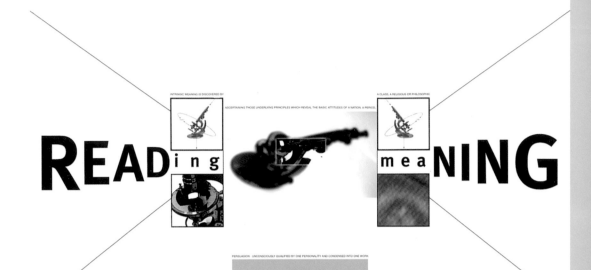

designer
Irma Boom

photographer
Aero photo Schiphol bv

design company
Irma Boom

country of origin
The Netherlands

work description
Telephone cards, with
their reverse images (far
right) combined to form a
picture

dimensions
shown actual size
85 x 54 mm
3⅜ x 2⅛ in

92

Telekom Telefonkarte

LÄNGS RISSIGER GRÜFTE GLEITET DURCH DIE PURPURNE
LANDSCHAFT DER RHEIN - **BERTUS AAFJES**

DEZE TELEFOONKAART IS OOK TE
GEBRUIKEN IN DUITSLAND

ZIE IK. HOE LANGS KROCHTEN EN SPLETEN DE RIJN
DOOR HET PAARS LANDSCHAP GLIJDT - BERTUS AAFJES

ptt telecom   A401120305

Telekom Telefonkarte

ICH WILL EIN WORT, DAS ZAUBERN KANN
UND ZAUBERT, DAB DU BEI MIR BIST **VASALIS**

DEZE TELEFOONKAART IS OOK TE
GEBRUIKEN IN DUITSLAND

IK WIL EEN WOORD, DAT TOOVREN KAN
EN TOOVERT, DAT JE BIJ MIJ BENT - VASALIS

ptt telecom   B400970701

designer
Brad Trost

photographer
Kurt Hettle

art director
Brad Trost

design company
doubledagger

country of origin
USA

work description
Promotional postcard for
Herron Photo Lab

dimensions
195 x 126 mm
7³⁄₅ x 6 in

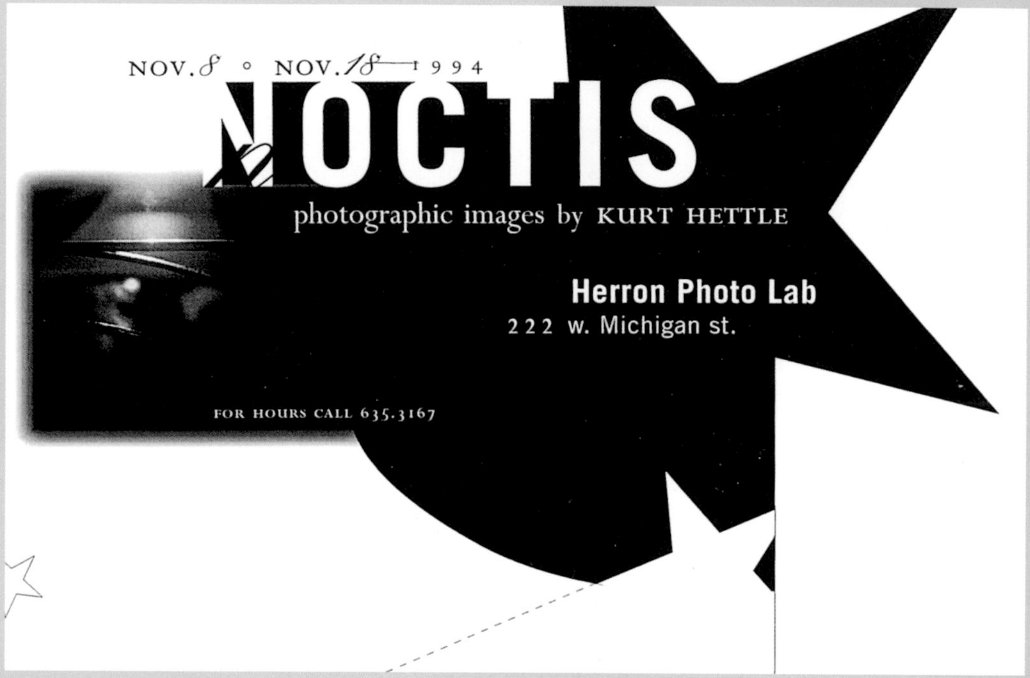

94

designer
Elisabeth Charman

photographer
Elisabeth Charman

art director
Elisabeth Charman

design company
doubledagger

country of origin
USA

work description
Gold Star Heaven, a self-
promotional postcard

dimensions
152 x 102 mm
5 x 4 in

95

designer
Mark Hough

art director
Jane Kosstrin-Yurick

design company
Doublespace

country of origin
USA

work description
Poster for the Dartmouth
College Conference

dimensions
580 x 430 mm
22⁷/₈ x 16⁷/₈ in

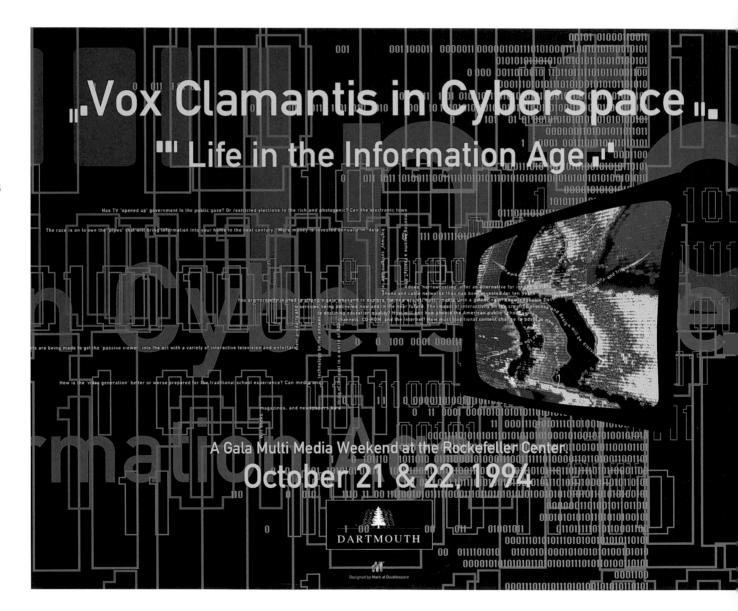

designer
Chris Myers

photographer
Chris Myers

art director
Nancy Mayer

design company
Mayer & Myers

country of origin
USA

work description
Lecture poster, for The
American Institute of
Graphic Arts, Philadelphia,
and the University of the
Arts, Philadelphia

dimensions
482 x 482 mm
19 x 19 in

designers
Stephanie Krieger
Maximilian Sztatecsny

photographer
right
Margherita Spiluttini

art director
Stephanie Krieger

design company
Krieger/Sztatecsny

country of origin
Austria

work description
Front covers of two
architecture booklets for
Architektur Zentrum Wien

dimensions
150 x 298 mm
5⅞ x 11¾ in

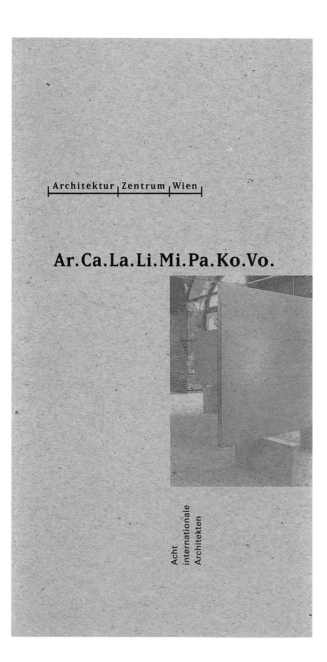

designer
Stephanie Krieger

photographer
Johannes Faber

art director
Stephanie Krieger

design company
Krieger/Sztatecsny

country of origin
Austria

work description
Spreads from leaflets
announcing the fourth
and fifth Viennese
Seminars on Architecture,
for Architektur Zentrum
Wien

dimensions
210 x 148 mm
8¼ x 5⅞ in

designers
Christopher Ashworth
Amanda Sissons
Neil Fletcher
John Holden
Dave Smith

photographer
John Holden

art director
Christopher Ashworth

design company
Invisible

country of origin
UK

work description
Jacket of *Interference*,
a book exploring the
dehumanizing and
sinister effects of security
surveillance in the city,
published by Ümran
projects

dimensions
668 x 290 mm
26¼ x 11⅜ in

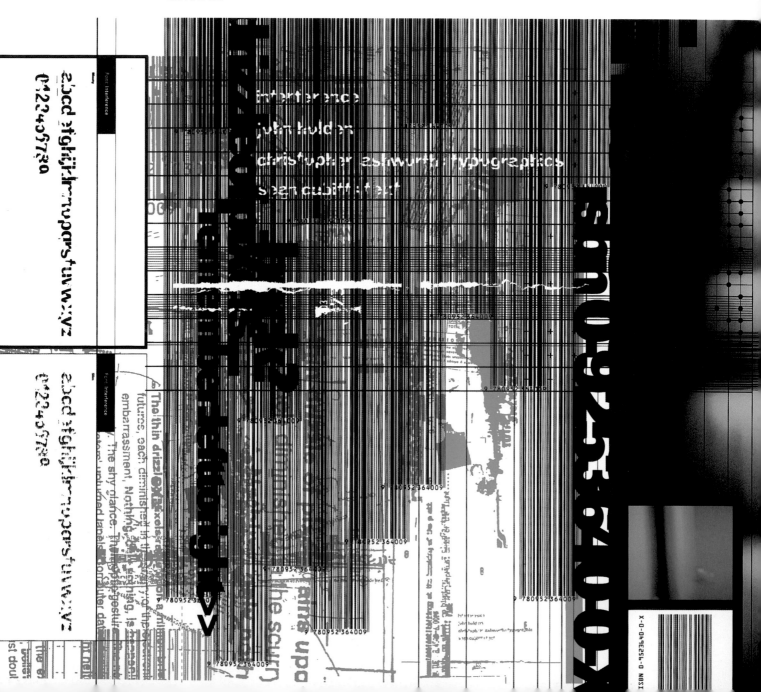

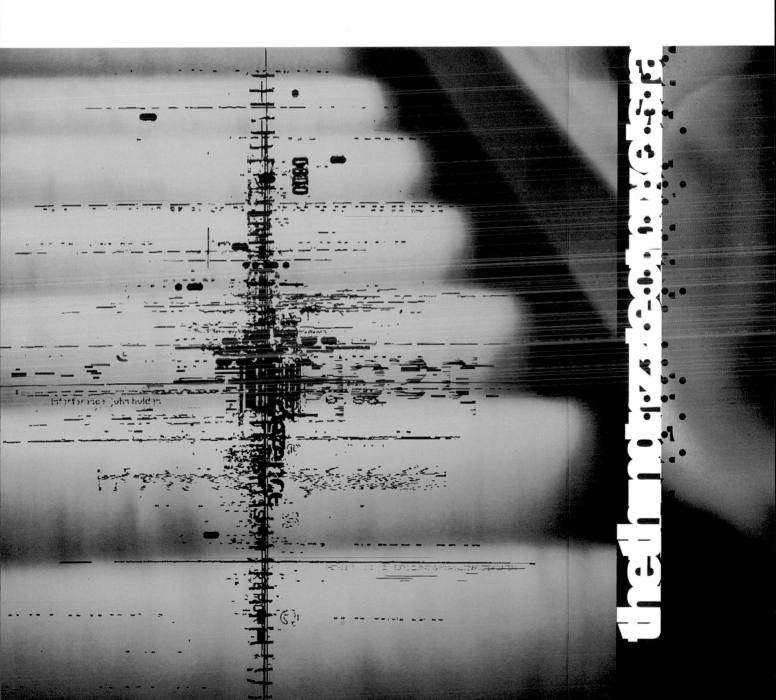

designer
Naomi Mizusaki

photographer
Jennifer Lynch

art directors
Drew Hodges
Vincent Sainato
Elisa Feinman

design company
Spot Design

country of origin
USA

work description
Box (left) and spreads
from a sci-fi channel
marketing planner; the
spreads are interleaved
with sheets of translucent
red gel which obscure
areas of the graphics or
words to create additional
messages

dimensions
299 x 171 mm
11¾ x 6¾ in

BLASTING OFF

The Sci-Fi Channel is the interstellar source for a most diverse mix of science fiction entertainment. All Sci-Fi Channel offerings are suitable for family viewing, appealing to viewers of all ages – men, women, teens, kids, general viewers and intense sci-fi fans!

Cable subscribers turn to the Sci-Fi Channel for inventive science fiction fare they can't find anywhere else in the galaxy...

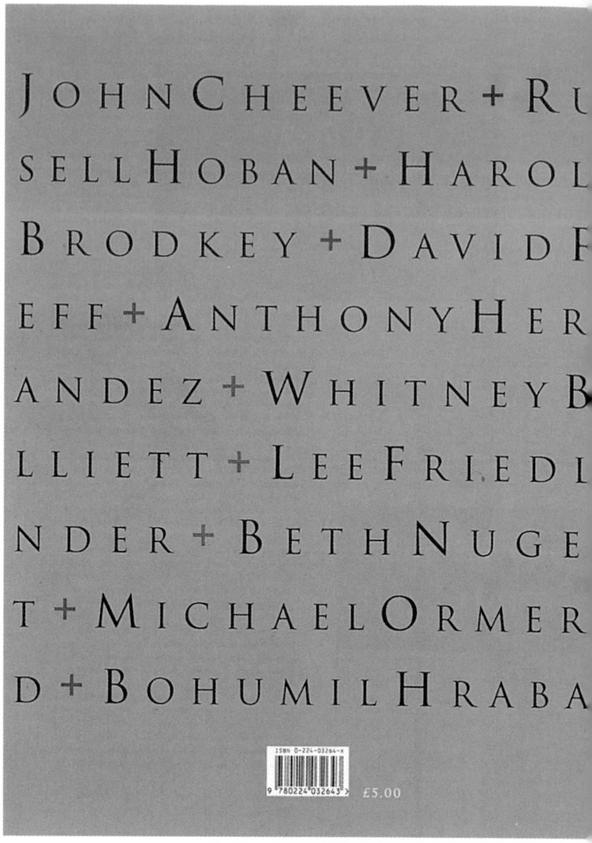

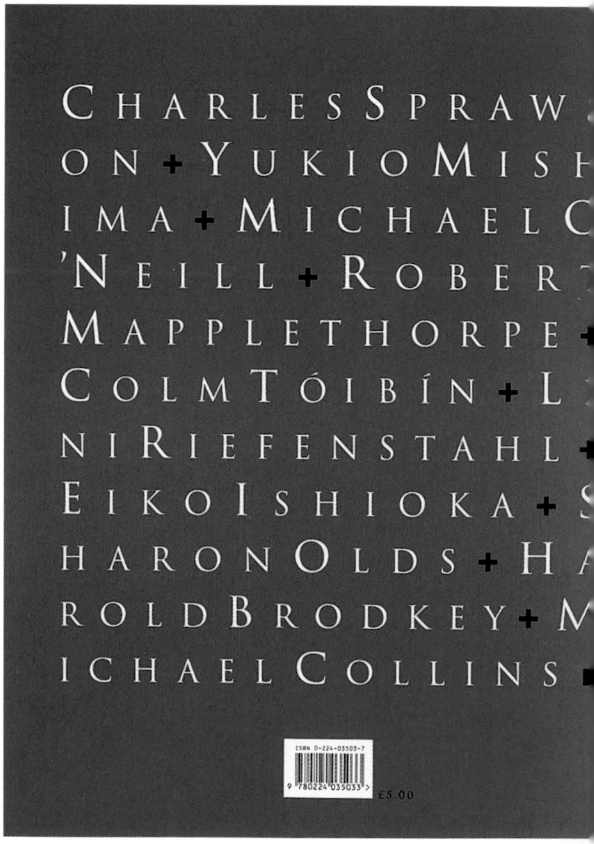

designers
Peter Dyer
Conor Brady

photographer
Michael Ormerod

design company
React

country of origin
UK

work description
Front and back covers of
the magazine *Cape*, issues
2 & 3

dimensions
274 x 362 mm
10¾ x 14¼ in

104

JOHN CHEEVER + RU
SELL HOBAN + HAROL
BRODKEY + DAVID F
EFF + ANTHONY HER
ANDEZ + WHITNEY B
LLIETT + LEE FRIEDL
NDER + BETH NUGE
T + MICHAEL ORMER
D + BOHUMIL HRABA

CHARLES SPRAW
ON + YUKIO MISH
IMA + MICHAEL O
'NEILL + ROBER
MAPPLETHORPE +
COLM TÓIBÍN + L
NI RIEFENSTAHL +
EIKO ISHIOKA + S
HARON OLDS + HA
ROLD BRODKEY + M
ICHAEL COLLINS

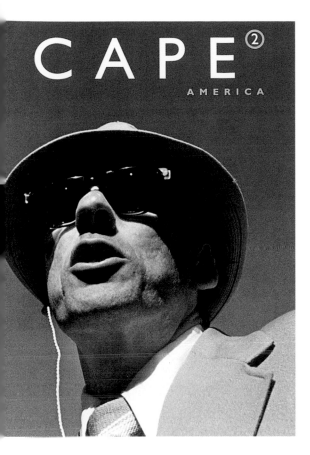

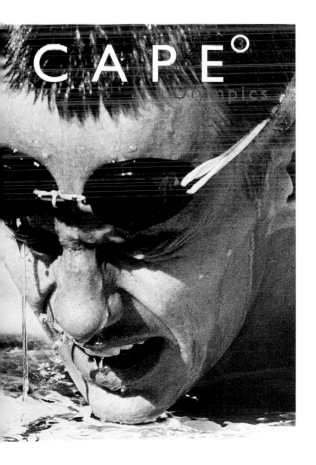

designers

this page

Jonathan Barnbrook
(above)

David Ellis (below)

opposite page

Andy Altmann (left)

Phil Baines (center)

Chris Priest (far right)

106

design company

Why Not Associates

country of origin

UK

work description

Yak 2, posters

dimensions

this page

762 x 508 mm

30 x 20 in

opposite page

508 x 762 mm

20 x 30 in

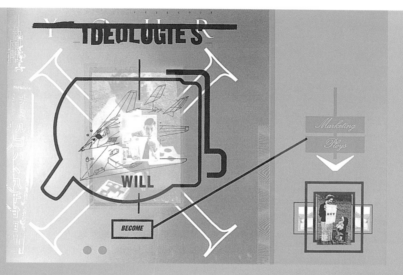

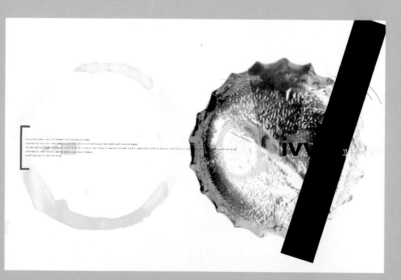

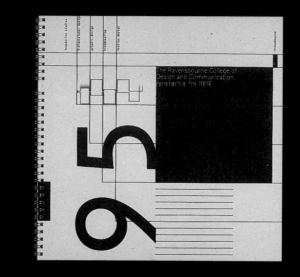

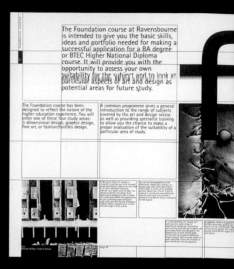

designers
Rupert Bassett
Paul Blackburn

photographer
Ringan Ledwidge

country of origin
UK

work description
Cover, spreads, and
pages from the 1995
catalog/prospectus for
Ravensbourne College
of Design and
Communication,
Chislehurst

dimensions
300 x 285 mm
11 7/8 x 11 1/4 in

108

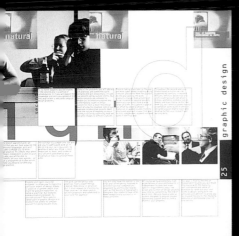

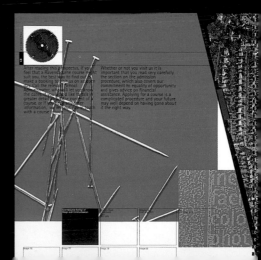

four

fac ilities

post graduate study

professional resource

3-dimensional des

21

Ravensbourne offers courses in foundation studies, 3-dimensional design, graphic design, broadcasting and fashion design.

natural

graphic design

25

After reading this prospectus, if you feel that a Ravensbourne course might suit you, the best way to find out is to make a booking to see us on an Open Day. Call the relevant School Administrator who will let you know the dates we have and like to talk in greater detail about the content of a course, or if you require other information, please contact us with a course tutor.

Whether or not you visit us it is important that you read very carefully the section on the admission procedure, which also covers our commitment to equality of opportunity and gives advice on financial assistance. Applying for a course is a complicated procedure and your future may well depend on having gone about it the right way.

designer
Nick Bell

art director
Jeremy Hall

design company
Nick Bell

country of origin
UK

work description
Ultraviolet series of CDs,
with an advertising
poster, for Virgin Classics

dimensions
CDs
120 x 120 mm
4¾ x 4¾ in
poster
594 x 840 mm
23⅜ x 33⅛ in

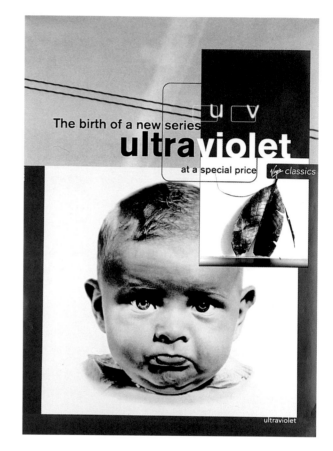

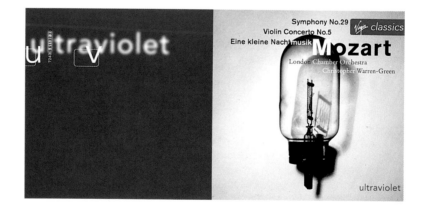

Mathis der Maler
Symphonic Metamorphoses
Hindemith
Bamberger Symphoniker
Karl Anton Rickenbacher

ultraviolet

Chants d'Auvergne
Canteloube
Arleen Auger   English Chamber Orchestra
Yan Pascal Tortelier

ultraviolet

Symphony No.1 Classical   Sinfonietta
Milhaud: La Création du monde
Prokofiev
Orchestre de Chambre de Lausanne
Alberto Zedda

ultraviolet

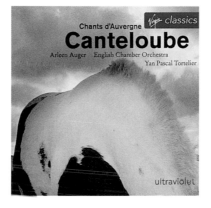

Pictures from an Exhibition
A Night on the Bare Mountain
Mussorgsky
Royal Liverpool Philharmonic Orchestra
Sir Charles Mackerras

ultraviolet

The Brandenburg Concertos
J S Bach
Scottish Ensemble   Jonathan Rees

ultraviolet

111

Adams   Glass   Reich   Heath
Minimalist
London Chamber Orchestra   Christopher Warren-Green

ultraviolet

Symphonies 40 & 41 Jupiter
Mozart
Sinfonia Varsovia   Yehudi Menuhin

ultraviolet

Symphony No.10   Festival Overture
Shostakovich
The London Philharmonic
Andrew Litton

ultraviolet

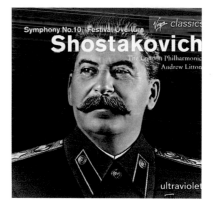

designers
Jason Edwards
Tim Hutchinson

college
Royal College of Art,
London

country of origin
UK

work description
Visual research project

dimensions
485 x 415 mm
19 1/8 x 16 3/4 in

112

designer
Jeremy Francis Mende

photographer
Jeremy Francis Mende

college
Cranbrook Academy
of Art, Michigan

country of origin
USA

work description
Pages from a proposed
large format book,
*Archilochus: The Severity
of his Satire*, an allegory
exploring the mental
interstices between
developmental stages in
adulthood

dimensions
381 x 559 mm
15 x 22 in

114

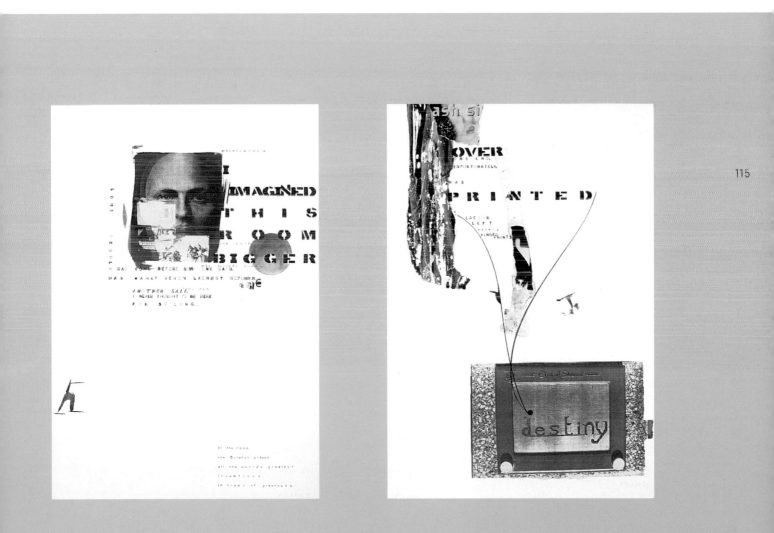

designer
Jennifer E. Moody

college
California Institute of
the Arts

country of origin
USA

work description
Furniture show poster

dimensions
711 x 1016 mm
28 x 40 in

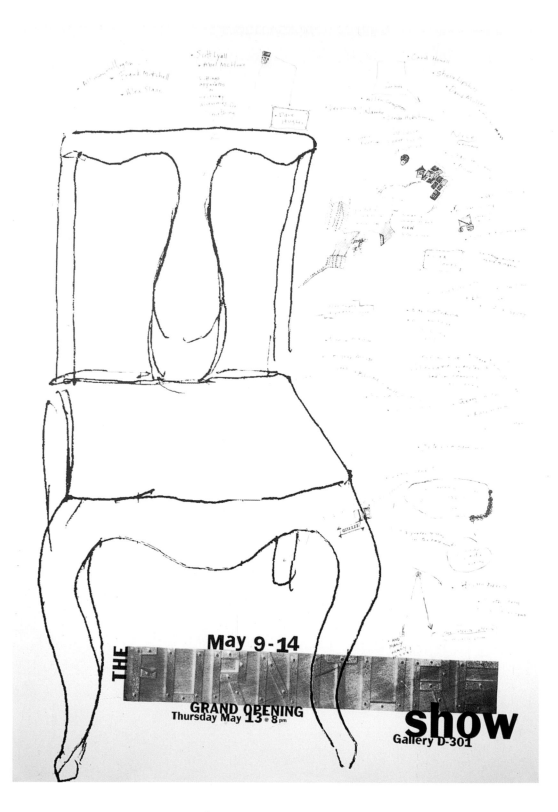

designer
Koeweiden/Postma
Associates

photographer
René Kramers

country of origin
The Netherlands

work description
Letterhead for René
Kramers Photography

dimensions
shown actual size
210 x 297 mm
8¼ x 11¾ in

designer
Jeff Düngfelder

illustrator
Jeff Düngfelder

art director
Jeff Düngfelder

design company
Studio DNA

country of origin
USA

work description
Self-promotional poster

dimensions
241 x 419 mm
9½ x 16½ in

designer
Mark Diaper

photographer
Richard Foster

design company
Lippa Pearce Design
Limited

country of origin
UK

work description
Front cover and fold-out
poster from an AIDS
awareness booklet for the
Terrence Higgins Trust on
World AIDS Day

dimensions
booklet
120 x 120 mm
1¾ x 1¾ in
fold-out poster
347 x 466 mm
13⅝ x 18⅜ in

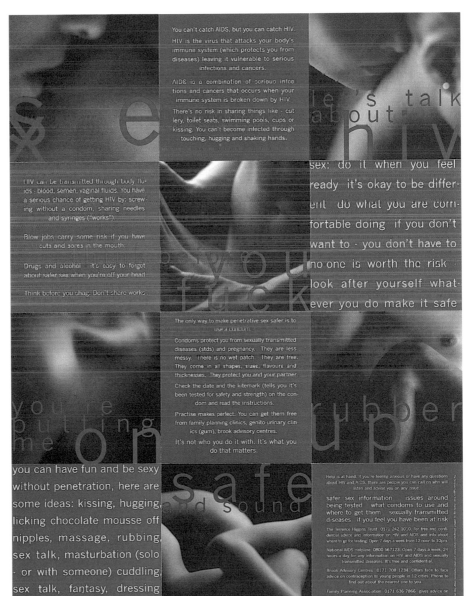

designer
Richard Horsford

college
Ravensbourne College
of Design and
Communication,
Chislehurst

tutor
Gill Scott

120 **country of origin**
UK

work description
A campaign poster (right),
with information form on
the reverse (far right), to
raise awareness of the
issues facing deaf and
dumb people

dimensions
this page
420 x 594 mm
16½ x 23⅜ in
opposite page
594 x 420 mm
23⅜ x 16½ in

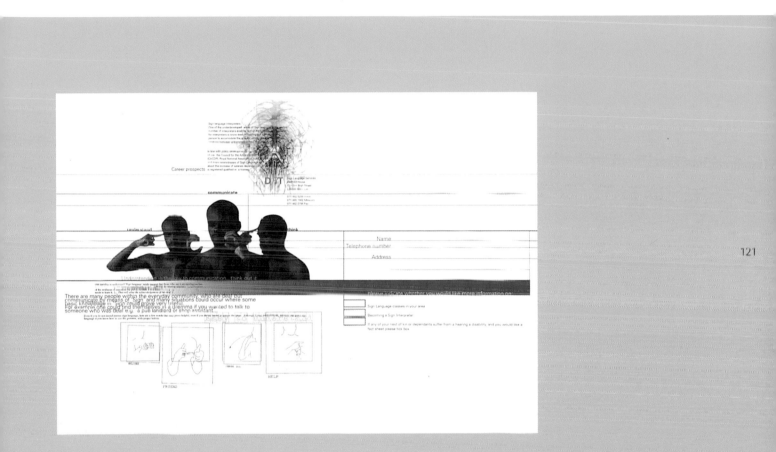

designer
Conor Brady

photographer
Conor Brady

design company
React

country of origin
UK

work description
Front cover and spine of
the book *Dreams of a
Final Theory*, for Vintage
publishers

dimensions
145 x 198 mm
5¾ x 7¾ in

designer
Conor Brady

photographer
Tim Simmons

design company
React

country of origin
UK

work description
Front cover and spine
of the book *Small is
Beautiful*, for Vintage
publishers

dimensions
145 x 198 mm
5¾ x 7¾ in

designer
Peter Dyer

photographer
Robert Clifford

design company
React

country of origin
UK

work description
Front cover of the book
The Acid House, for
Jonathan Cape publishers

dimensions
145 x 198 mm
5¾ x 7¾ in

designers
Peter Dyer
Conor Brady

photographer
Conor Brady

design company
React

country of origin
UK

work description
Front cover of the book
Europe: The Rough Guide,
for The Rough Guide
publishers

dimensions
145 x 198 mm
5¾ x 7¾ in

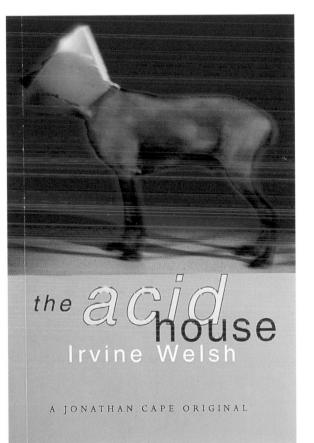

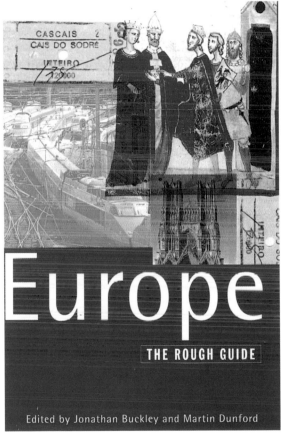

designer
Nick Bell

photographers
BBC Library
Nick Bell

art director
Roger Mann at
Casson Mann

design company
Nick Bell

124

country of origin
UK

work description
Design for manager's
office and department
reception at BBC Schools
Television: a typographic
skin to wrap around two
reception desks and to
cover the surface of a
freestanding storage wall

dimensions
each laminate sheet
1050 x 1250 mm
41⅜ x 49¼ in

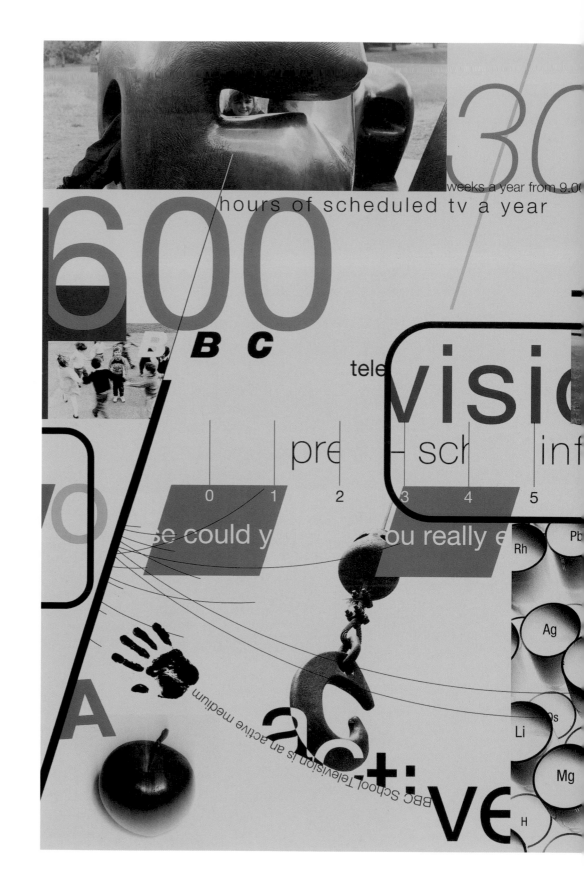

designers
Christopher Ashworth
Dave Smith

art director
Christopher Ashworth

design company
Invisible

country of origin
UK

126

work description
Four from a set of six
promotional postcards
for Depth Charge
Records

dimensions
shown actual size
149 x 100 mm
5⅞ x 3⅞ in

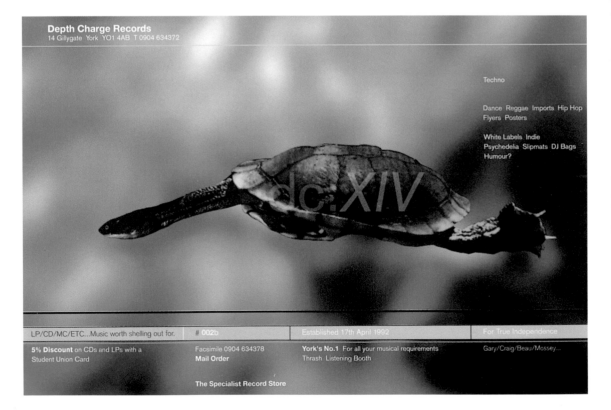

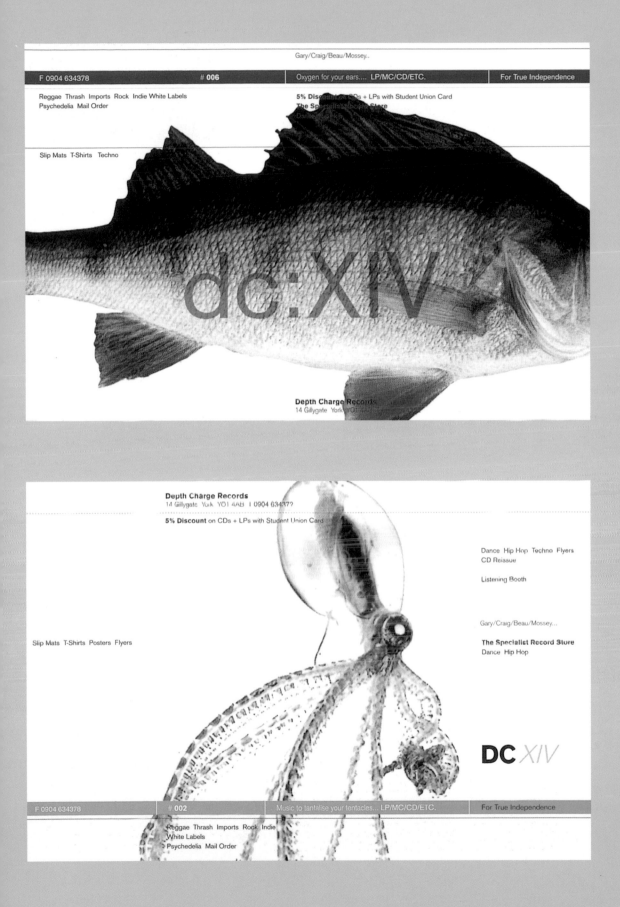

Gary/Craig/Beau/Mossey..

F 0904 634378 | # 006 | Oxygen for your ears.... LP/MC/CD/ETC. | For True Independence

Reggae Thrash Imports Rock Indie White Labels
Psychedelia Mail Order

5% Discount on CDs + LPs with Student Union Card
The Specialist Record Store

Slip Mats T-Shirts Techno

Depth Charge Records
14 Gillygate York YO1

Depth Charge Records
14 Gillygate York YO1 4AB 1 0904 634372

5% Discount on CDs + LPs with Student Union Card

Dance Hip Hop Techno Flyers
CD Reissue

Listening Booth

Gary/Craig/Beau/Mossey...

The Specialist Record Store
Dance Hip Hop

Slip Mats T-Shirts Posters Flyers

DC XIV

F 0904 634378 | # 002 | Music to tantalise your tentacles... LP/MC/CD/ETC. | For True Independence

Reggae Thrash Imports Rock Indie
White Labels
Psychedelia Mail Order

designer
Hans P. Brandt

design company
Total Design

country of origin
The Netherlands

work description
Hubble Space Telescope, a
poster for the European
Space Agency

dimensions
630 x 890 mm
24¾ x 35 in

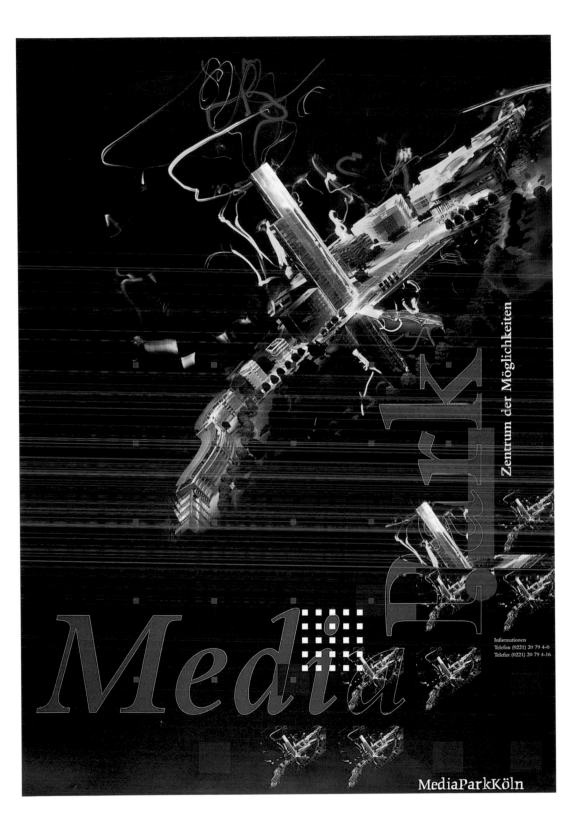

designer
Hans P. Brandt

photographer
Tom Miltemeijer

design company
Total Design

country of origin
The Netherlands

work description
MediaParkKöln, a poster

dimensions
597 x 850 mm
23½ x 33½ in

129

designers
Nilesh Mehta
Uday Patel

college
Ravensbourne College
of Design and
Communication,
Chislehurst

country of origin
UK

work description
Spread from a booklet
displaying the answers
given by people of various
ages and cultures to ten
questions posed by the
designers/publishers

dimensions
295 x 418 mm
11⅝ x 16½ in

bulb = light   water = growth

0.1 A dulcimer, which I handmade some fifteen years ago and which has given me many moments of pleasure.

0.2 In 1969, on the top deck of an oil tanker in the Indian Ocean, at night. When I first lost and found myself, looking at the waves.

0.3 Being unable to cope.

0.4 Fear of something different to oneself.

0.5 Yes, because I think one should aspire to something greater than oneself. That is what I consider religion to be.

0.6 Abolish money, and make myself president of the world!

0.7 My first girlfriend, who is still a friend after twenty seven years.

0.8 Yes, most people I know including myself have experienced drugs.

0.9 I don't have a favourite joke. Jokes are usually demeaning other people in someway, or things or.. I don't like jokes. I like teasing or playing with words.

0.10 Spend it!

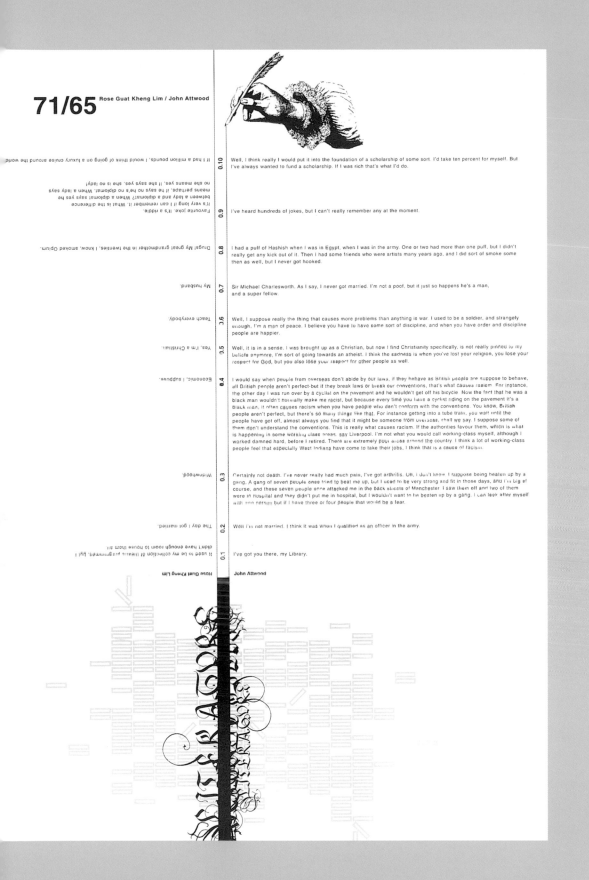

0.10 — If I had a million pounds, I would think of going on a luxury cruise around the world.

Well, I think really I would put it into the foundation of a scholarship of some sort. I'd take ten percent for myself. But I've always wanted to fund a scholarship. If I was rich that's what I'd do.

0.9 — Favourite joke. It's a riddle. It's very long if I can remember it. What is the difference between a lady and a diplomat? When a diplomat says yes he means perhaps, if he says no he's no diplomat. When a lady says no she means yes, if she says yes, she is no lady!

I've heard hundreds of jokes, but I can't really remember any at the moment.

0.8 — Drugs! My great grandmother in the twenties, I know, smoked Opium.

I had a puff of Hashish when I was in Egypt, when I was in the army. One or two had more than one puff, but I didn't really get any kick out of it. Then I had some friends who were artists many years ago, and I did sort of smoke some then as well, but I never got hooked.

0.7 — My husband.

Sir Michael Charlesworth. As I say, I never got married. I'm not a poof, but it just so happens he's a man, and a super fellow.

0.6 — Teach everybody.

Well, I suppose really the thing that causes more problems than anything is war. I used to be a soldier, and strangely enough, I'm a man of peace. I believe you have to have some sort of discipline, and when you have order and discipline people are happier.

0.5 — Yes, I'm a Christian.

Well, it is in a sense. I was brought up as a Christian, but now I find Christianity specifically, is not really pinned to my beliefs anymore. I'm sort of going towards an atheist. I think the sadness is when you've lost your religion, you lose your respect for God, but you also lose your respect for other people as well.

0.4 — Economic, I suppose.

I would say when people from overseas don't abide by our laws, if they behave as British people are suppose to behave, all British people aren't perfect-but if they break laws or break our conventions, that's what causes racism. For instance, the other day I was run over by a cyclist on the pavement and he wouldn't get off his bicycle. Now the fact that he was a black man wouldn't normally make me racist, but because every time you have a cyclist riding on the pavement it's a black man, it often causes racism when you have people who don't conform with the conventions. You know, British people aren't perfect, but there's so many things like that. For instance getting into a tube train, you wait until the people have got off, almost always you find that it might be someone from overseas, shall we say. I suppose some of them don't understand the conventions. This is really what causes racism. If the authorities favour them, which is what is happening in some working class areas, say Liverpool. I'm not what you would call working-class myself, although I worked damned hard, before I retired. There are extremely poor areas around the country. I think a lot of working-class people feel that especially West Indians have come to take their jobs, I think that is a cause of racism.

0.3 — Widowhood.

Certainly not death. I've never really had much pain, I've got arthritis. Oh, I don't know. I suppose being beaten up by a gang. A gang of seven people once tried to beat me up, but I used to be very strong and fit in those days, and I'm big of course, and these seven people once attacked me in the back streets of Manchester. I saw them off and two of them were in hospital and they didn't put me in hospital, but I wouldn't want to be beaten up by a gang. I can look after myself with one person but if I have three or four people that would be a fear.

0.2 — The day I got married.

Well I'm not married. I think it was when I qualified as an officer in the army.

0.1 — It used to be my collection of literature and grammars, but I didn't have enough room to house them all.

I've got you there, my Library.

Rose Guat Kheng Lim   John Attwood

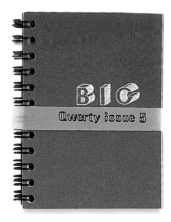

designer
Stephen Banham

art director
Stephen Banham

design company
The Letterbox

country of origin
Australia

work description
Front cover and spreads
from the magazine
Qwerty, issue 5

dimensions
80 x 105 mm
3⅛ x 4⅛ in

Feet	Metres	Points
25	8	2275

All I was given was a street-map reference
and the promise of something very exciting
indeed. Always inclined to take up such an
offer, I followed the instructions which led
me into the deep industrial heartland of
Richmond. I stood on the spot marked X on
the map and wondered what it was about.
I slowly looked up and there it was. The
biggest upper case K I had ever laid my
eyes on. This type, despite its scale, was
obscured from distant view by the buildings
that had since been built around it.

Feet	Metres	Points
10	3.5	995

Like a bright glowing red signature atop the mock castle architecture of the building's facade, the Astoria taxi sign would have to be the best loved lower case a in Melbourne (for those of us who concern ourselves with such things). Its spontaneous scribble-like form somehow runs contrary to its physical size and complexity of construction.

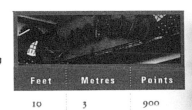

Feet	Metres	Points
10	3	900

This typographic drag queen is possibly the most recognisable in Melbourne. Its scale and sense of occasion beckons the viewer inward asking you to politely ignore its crumbling facade.

133

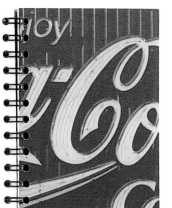

Feet	Metres	Points
40	13	3698

Situated in Sydney's King Cross, the largest C is predictably that of a Coca Cola Sign. One of the most famous over-sized members of our alphabet, this sign is seen by approximately 28 million people each year.

For those interested in the structural details, it contains 1.785 kilometres of neon tube, and 5 kilometres of electrical cable. It is the largest backlit display in Australia.

Feet	Metres	Points
8	2.5	500

and what a Z to cap it all off.

This rare find (you'll know what I mean when you try to look for big Z's) is a wonderfully substantial one, adorning an otherwise bland building on Church Street, Richmond.

designer
Alan Chandler

country of origin
UK

work description
Spreads from
typographic
sketch books

dimensions
300 x 420 mm
11⅞ x 16½ in

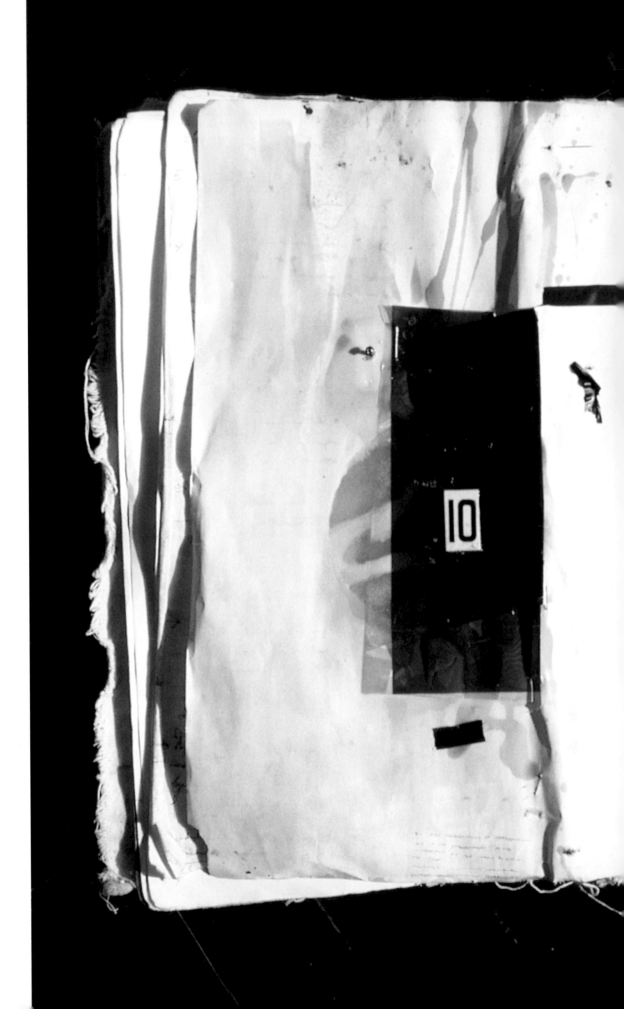

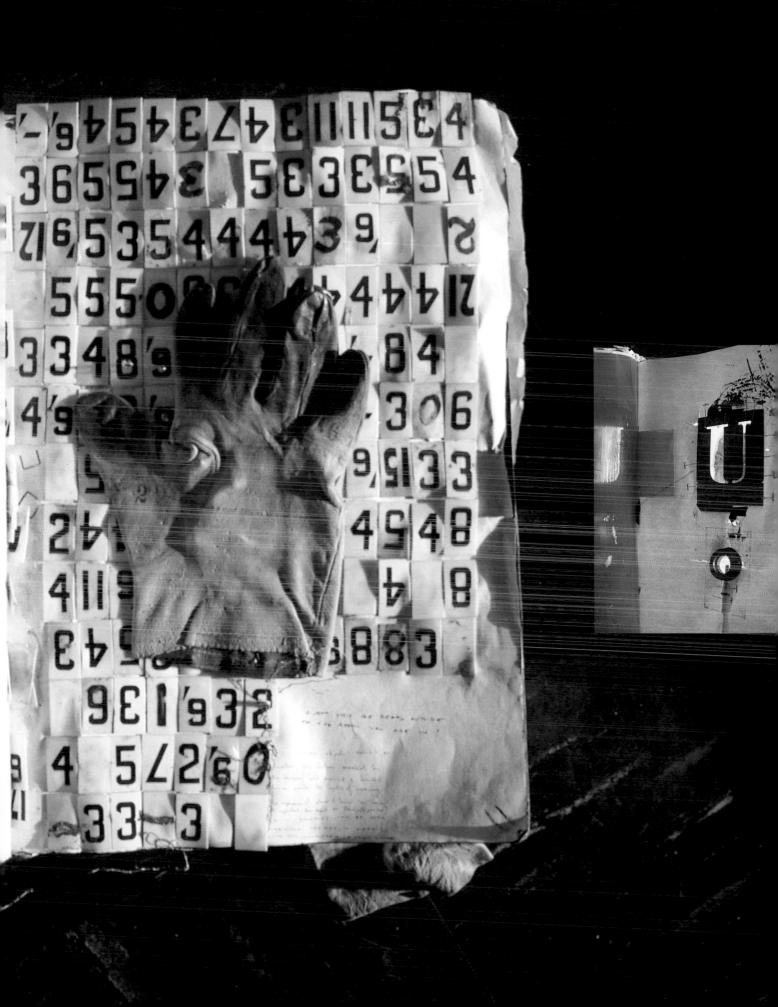

designers
Barbara Gluaber
Somi Kim

design company
Heavy Meta (Barbara
Gluaber)
ReVerb (Somi Kim)

photographer
Steven A. Gunther

country of origin
USA

work description
Spread and front cover
from a catalog/prospectus
for the California Institute
of the Arts

dimensions
200 x 285 mm
7⅞ x 11¼ in

136

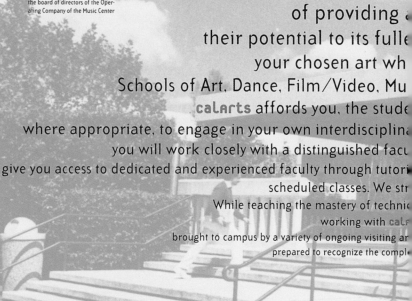

Steven D. Lavine became CalArts' third president in July of 1988. Before coming to CalArts, he was associate director for Arts and Humanities at the Rockefeller Foundation in New York City. There he provided leadership in the full spectrum of visual, performing and literary arts, with special emphasis on programs that challenge contemporary artists and cultural institutions to work toward an international and intercultural focus. While at the Rockefeller Foundation, he served on the board of directors of the Kitchen Center for Video,

Music, Dance, Performance, and Film and of the Mabou Mines Theater Collective. He was also a selection panelist for the INPUT Public Television Screening Conferences in Montreal, Canada and Granada, Spain.

He currently serves on the board of directors of the Los Angeles Philharmonic, the American Council for the Arts, and KCRW-FM National Public Radio, as well as the Governing Committee of the Institute for Advanced Study and Research in African Humanities at Northwestern University (for Northwestern and the Social Science Research Council), the Visiting Committee of the J. Paul Getty Museum, and the National Advisory Committee of the Smithsonian Institute's Experimental Gallery. He has served on the board of directors of the Operating Company of the Music Center

of Los Angeles, as co-director of the Arts and Government Program for the American Assembly at Columbia University, and co-chair of the Mayor's Working Group of the Los Angeles Theatre Centre. In 1991 he co-edited with Ivan Karp, *Exhibiting Cultures: The Poetics and Politics of Museum Display.* In 1992 the Smithsonian Institution Press released their second co-edited volume, *Museums and Communities: The Politics of Public Culture.*

of providing
their potential to its fulle
your chosen art wh
Schools of Art, Dance, Film/Video, Mu
calarts affords you, the stude
where appropriate, to engage in your own interdisciplina
you will work closely with a distinguished facu
give you access to dedicated and experienced faculty through tutori
scheduled classes. We str
While teaching the mastery of technic
working with calr
brought to campus by a variety of ongoing visiting ar
prepared to recognize the compl

STEVEN D. LAVINE, PRESIDENT

president's message

Throughout its history, caLArts
has been guided by its founding goal
vironment which enables emerging artists to develop
tent. At caLArts you can perfect skills in
ining knowledge of the other arts through our
eatre, and the Division of Critical Studies.
opportunity to forge new relationships among the arts, and,
lorations. ● At caLArts.
practicing artists. Innovative programs
ntoring, and independent studies as well as through regularly
n creativity and self-discipline.
strive to respond to your individual needs ● In addition to
lar faculty, you will have the opportunity to learn from many other distinguished artists
rams. ● As future artists, you must be
litical, social, and aesthetic questions and respond to them

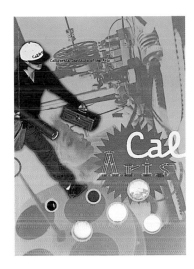

with informed, independent judgment. At caLArts, these abilities are fostered in the Division of Critical Studies as well as in the arts schools. The Critical Studies faculty of dedicated teachers and scholars will introduce you to the basic methods and disciplines of the liberal arts—the humanities, sciences, and social sciences—and especially to concerns of the arts and thought processes in the arts. This program will broaden your knowledge and understanding of the world and help you to analyze issues critically and imaginatively ● During your studies at caLArts, you will explore the philosophical, literary, social, and aesthetic dimensions of a diverse culture. You will meet and work with faculty, students, and visiting artists who represent various ethnic, cultural and national groups. Through our Community Arts Partnership (CAP), you will have the opportunity to work at cultural centers in neighborhoods throughout Los Angeles. ● As we consider caLArts' future, we see four immediate opportunities for enhancing the education we offer. The first is to continue to work toward including a broad range of voices—ethnic, cultural, and international—in every area of the Institute. The past decade has brought rapid change in this arena, but there is still a long road to travel, in the arts as in our society. The second is to make available the array of resources for interactive and multimedia artmaking. Integrated media technologies will create a firm platform for interdisciplinary exploration, the third area in which we hope to see development in the rest of this decade. caLArts was designed not only to offer the arts individually but to encourage interdisciplinary inquiry. As we enter our second quarter century, we are still challenged to fulfill this vision of our founders. Fourth, but not at all least among these priorities, is to strengthen the place of writing at caLArts. Recently, we've put in place an MFA program in Critical Writing/Arts Practice. Now we must work toward a full-scale writing program that takes advantage of the unique interdisciplinary resources at the Institute. ● During the two and one-half decades of its existence, caLArts has been, appropriately, in a continual state of evolution. These new initiatives recognize that the place of the arts in society is in constant flux, and so necessarily caLArts must change and develop. At caLArts our mandate is to help create the future; we invite you to join us in this adventure. *Steven D Lavine*

designer
Stephen Hyland

college
The Surrey Institute of
Art & Design, Farnham

tutor
Mike Ryan

country of origin
UK

work description
Spread from *Area 39*,
a magazine project
covering experimental
music, design, and
multimedia

dimensions
210 x 297 mm
8¼ x 11¾ in

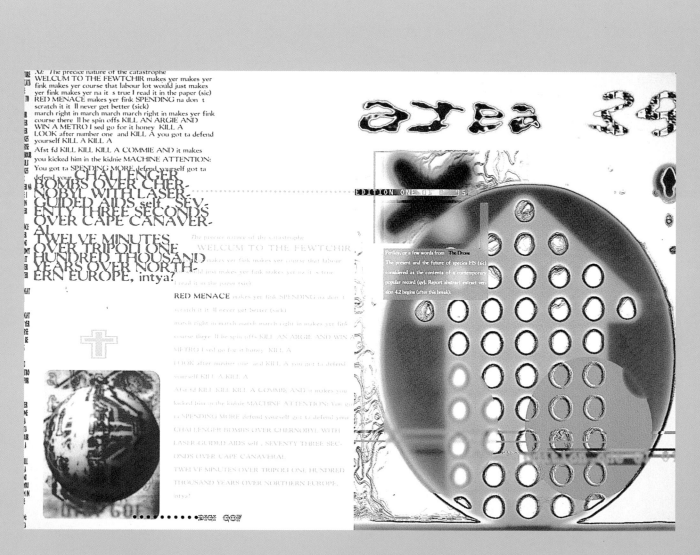

designer
Ed Telling

college
The Surrey Institute of
Art & Design, Farnham

tutor
Mike Ryan

country of origin
UK

work description
Spread from *Area 39*,
a magazine project
covering experimental
music, design, and
multimedia

dimensions
210 x 297 mm
8¼ x 11¾ in

designer
Naomi Mizusaki

art directors
Rosie Pisani
Pete Aguannd
Drew Hodges

design company
Spot Design

country of origin
USA

work description
Advertisements for the
Independent Film Channel

dimensions
200 x 152 mm
7⅞ x 6 in

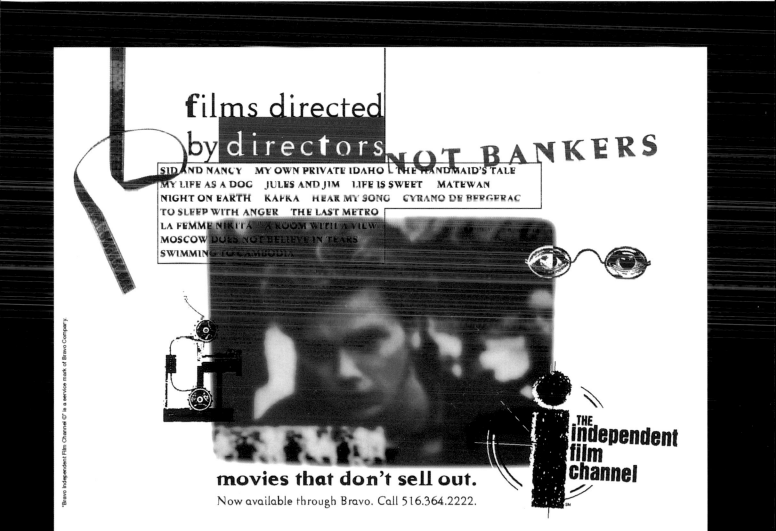

films directed by directors NOT BANKERS

SID AND NANCY   MY OWN PRIVATE IDAHO   THE HANDMAID'S TALE
MY LIFE AS A DOG   JULES AND JIM   LIFE IS SWEET   MATEWAN
NIGHT ON EARTH   KAFKA   HEAR MY SONG   CYRANO DE BERGERAC
TO SLEEP WITH ANGER   THE LAST METRO
LA FEMME NIKITA   A ROOM WITH A VIEW
MOSCOW DOES NOT BELIEVE IN TEARS
SWIMMING TO CAMBODIA

movies that don't sell out.
Now available through Bravo. Call 516.364.2222.

THE independent film channel

designer
Vincent Sainato

photographer
Mark Hill

art director
Drew Hodges

design company
Spot Design

country of origin
USA

142

work description
Page from the 1994
Hanna-Barbera
*Flintstones Collectibles
Calendar*

dimensions
280 x 660 mm
11 x 26 in

designer
George Plesko

photographer
George Plesko
Tom Davies

art director
Nancy Mayer

design company
Mayer & Myers

country of origin
USA

143

work description
Page from *The University of the Arts Calendar and Student Handbook*, for The University of the Arts, Philadelphia

dimensions
277 x 425 mm
10⅞ x 16¾ in

designer
Richard Shanks

college
California Institute
of the Arts

country of origin
USA

work description
Pages from *Shoes Make The Man*, a false diary
that is a self-authored
experimental typography
project exploring cultural
identity and stereotype

144

dimensions
254 x 381 mm
10 x 15 in

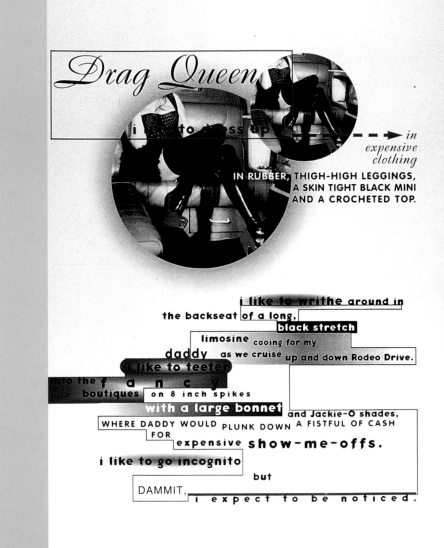

designer
Russell Warren-Fisher

design company
Warren-Fisher

country of origin
UK

work description
Spread and cover from a
brochure for Camilla
Arthur, shown with the
promotional envelope

dimensions
brochure
320 x 255 mm
12⅝ x 10 in
envelope
380 x 300 mm
15 x 11⅞ in

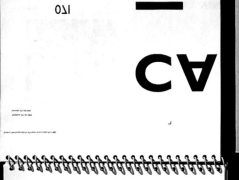

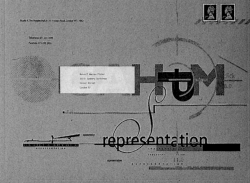

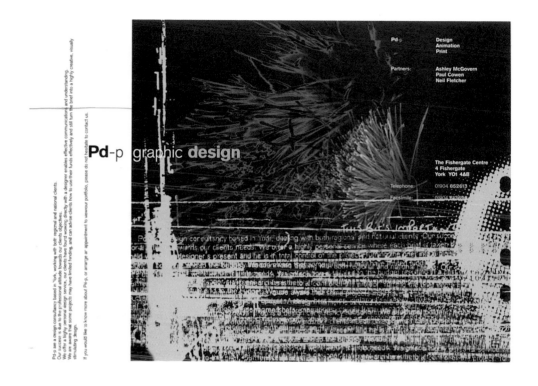

Pd-p graphic **design**

Pd-p are a design consultancy based in York, working with both regional and national clients.
Our success is due to the professional attitude towards our clients objectives.
We offer a highly personal design service, our clients have found working directly with a designer enables effective communications and understanding. We are aware that some projects may have limited funding, and can advise clients how to use their funds effectively and still turn the brief into a highly creative, visually stimulating design.

If you would like to know more about Pd-p, or arrange an appointment to view our portfolio, please do not hesitate to contact us.

designer
Neil Fletcher

design company
Pd-p

country of origin
UK

work description
Self-promotional
postcards

dimensions
210 x 148 mm
8¼ x 5⅞ in

147

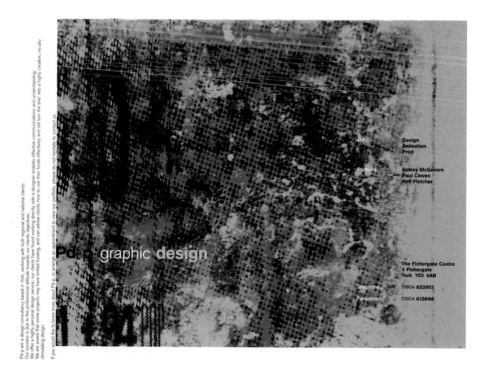

Pd-p graphic **design**

Pd-p are a design consultancy based in York, working with both regional and national clients.
Our success is due to the professional attitude towards our clients objectives.
We offer a highly personal design service, our clients have found working directly with a designer enables effective communications and understanding. We are aware that some projects may have limited funding, and can advise clients how to use their funds effectively and still turn the brief into a highly creative, visually stimulating design.

If you would like to know more about Pd-p, or arrange an appointment to view our portfolio, please do not hesitate to contact us.

designer
Cathy Rediehs Schaefer

art director
Tom Geismar

design company
Chermayeff & Geismar
Inc.

country of origin
USA

148

work description
Front cover and spreads
from a brochure
launching a reorganized
office furniture company,
the Knoll Group

dimensions
279 x 279 mm
11 x 11 in

Planning and furnishing the workplace today means thinking far beyond metal, wood and plastic. The people who work are changing, and so are the tools that they use. Demographic trends, leaps in computer and communications technology, reconfigured organizational structures, new sensitivity to workers' well-being and the environment —all make the workplace a focal point for unfamiliar and complex concerns. At **Knoll,** a company uniquely founded on the concept of **design,** we are redefining form and function to accommodate these new dimensions.

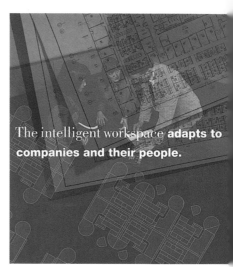

The intelligent workspace **adapts to companies and their people.**

intelligent workspace **supports the rk process.**

Knoll embodies a heritage of design and

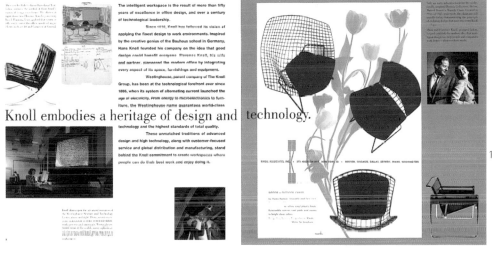

technology.

The intelligent workspace is the result of more than fifty years of excellence in office design, and over a century of technological leadership.

Since 1938, Knoll has followed its vision of applying the finest design to work environments. Inspired by the creative genius of the Bauhaus school in Germany, Hans Knoll founded his company on the idea that good design could benefit everyone. Florence Knoll, his wife and partner, pioneered the modern office by integrating every aspect of its space, furnishings and equipment.

Westinghouse, parent company of The Knoll Group, has been at the technological forefront ever since 1886, when its system of alternating current launched the age of electricity. From energy to microelectronics to furniture, the Westinghouse name guarantees world-class technology and the highest standards of total quality.

These unmatched traditions of advanced design and high technology, along with customer-focused service and global distribution and manufacturing, stand behind the Knoll commitment to create workspaces where people can do their best work and enjoy doing it.

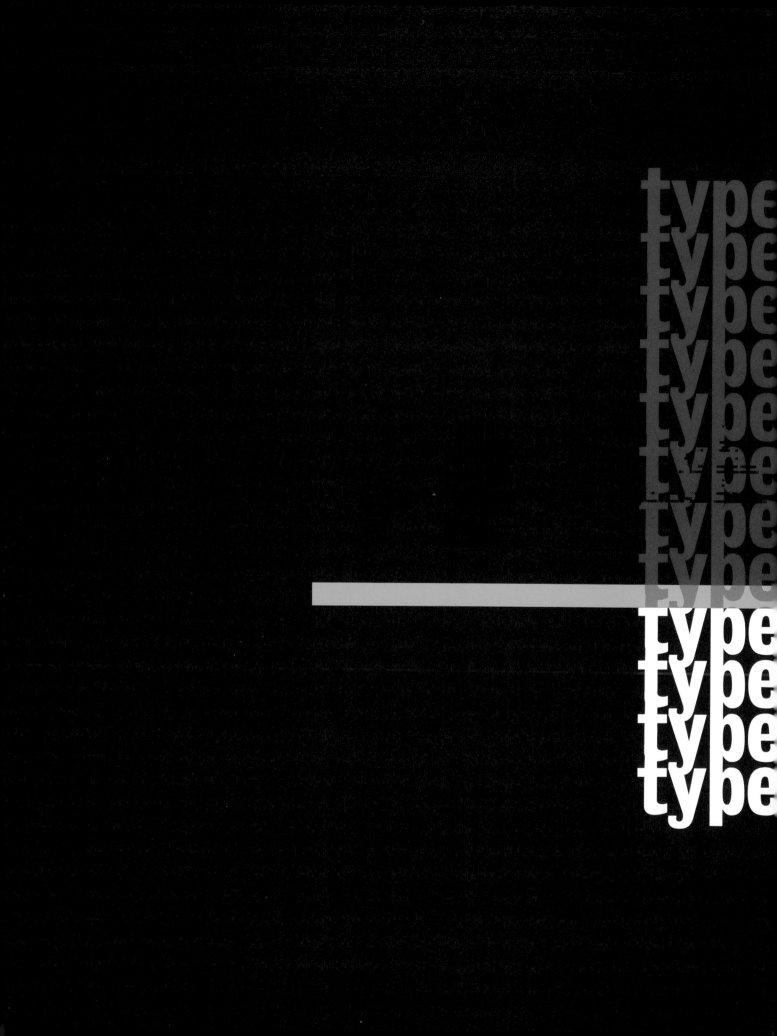

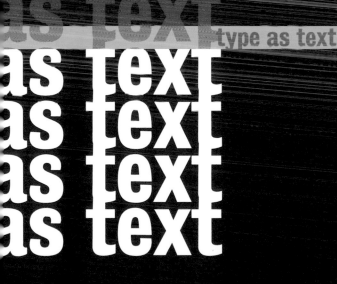

type as text

152

designer
Kees van Drongelen
(with cooperation from
Christine Baart and Harco
van den Hurk)

design company
Post & Van Drongelen,
VisualSpace

country of origin
The Netherlands

work description
Title page and spreads
from the book *The
Invisible in Architecture*,
for Academy Editions

dimensions
250 x 305 mm
9⅞ x 12 in

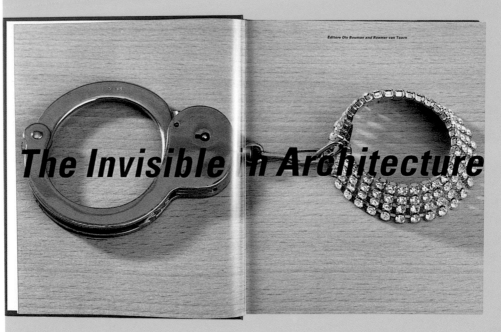

designers
Rudy VanderLans
Gail Swanlund

art director
Rudy VanderLans

design company
Emigre Graphics

country of origin
USA

work description
Spreads from *Emigre*
magazine, issue 32

dimensions
282 x 425 mm
11⅛ x 16¾ in

154

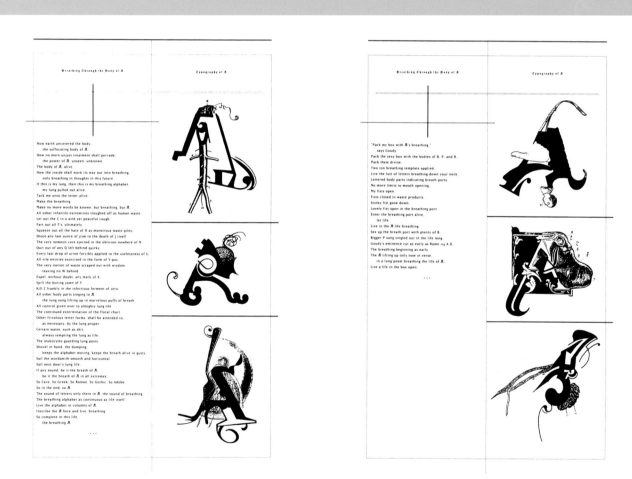

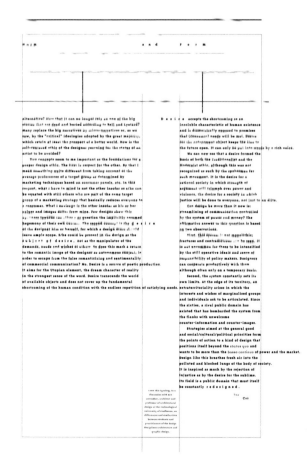

and form

alternative? Now that it can no longer rely on one of the big stories that are dead and buried according to Bell and Lyotard? Many replace the big narratives by micro-narratives or, as we saw, by the "critical" ideologies adopted by the great majority, which retain at least the prospect of a better world. How is the self-centred ethic of the designer yearning for the status of an artist to be avoided?

Two concepts seem to me important as the foundations for a proper design ethic. The first is respect for the other. By that I mean something quite different from taking account of the average preferences of a target group as determined by marketing techniques based on consumer panels, etc. In this respect, what I have in mind is not the other insofar as s/he can be equated with still others who are part of the same target group of a marketing strategy that basically reduces everyone to a consumer. What I envisage is the other insofar as his or her wishes and images differ from mine. Few designs show this as they move towards the other or question the implicitly assumed hegemony of their own desires. The second concept is the desire of the designer him or herself, for which a design must at least leave ample scope. S/he could be present in the design as the subject of desire, not as the manipulator of the demands, needs and wishes of others. Does this mark a return to the romantic image of the designer as autonomous subject, in order to escape from the false romanticizing and sentimentality of commercial communication? No. Desire is a source of poetic production. It aims for the Utopian element, the dream character of reality in the strongest sense of the word. Desire transcends the world of available objects and does not cover up the fundamental shortcoming of the human condition with the endless repetition of satisfying needs.

Desire accepts the shortcoming as an insoluble characteristic of human existence and is dialectically opposed to promises that (consumer) needs will be met. Desire for the entrepreneur object keeps the line to the future open. It can only be put into words by a rich voice.

We can now see that a desire formed the basis of both the traditionalist and the Modernist ethic, although this was not recognised as such by the spokesman for each movement. It is the desire for a rational society in which strength of argument will triumph over power and violence, the desire for a society in which justice will be done to everyone, not just to an élite.

Can design be more than it now is: streamlining of communication controlled by the system of power and money? The affirmative answer to this question is based on two observations.

First, this system is not monolithic; fractures and contradictions can be seen. It is not uncommon for these to be intensified by the still operative ideals and sense of responsibility of policy makers. Designers can cooperate productively with them although often only on a temporary basis.

Second, the system constantly sets its own limits. At the edge of its territory, an extraterritoriality arises in which the interests and wishes of marginalised groups and individuals ask to be articulated. Since the sixties, a rival public domain has existed that has bombarded the system from the flanks with unwelcome counter-information and counter-images.

Strategies aimed at the general good and social/cultural/political priorities form the points of action to a kind of design that positions itself beyond the status quo and wants to be more than the homo continuo of power and the market. Design like this breathes fresh air into the polluted and blocked lungs of the body of society. It is inspired as much by the rejection of injustice as by the desire for the sublime. Its field is a public domain that must itself be constantly redesigned.

The Can

ROUTE 666
TRANSGRESSING
THE
INFORMATION
SUPERHIGHWAY
BY PUICH TU

When I was 8,

I fixed a toaster that all others had given up on, including my much older brothers, all of whom were or wo   uld soon be engineers. It c   **THIS STORY IS TRUE**   ould have been that the mere   fact of taking it apart and putting it back together one more time had done the trick, or it could have been that going strictly on the visual patterns the wires made, I had seen something not quite right and repatterned it. In any case, we used that toaster for another few years. No one ever mentioned that I fixed it—that was taboo.

In fact, I got quite a verbal whapping for playing with "dangerous adult things, things t at could hurt" me. Where I had a great deal o pride in fixing the thing, sharing that fact at the dinner table led only to disaster. They j st thought I was a dumb little kid who wouldn't know any better than to stick bobby pins into a light socket. I got the scolding of my life, and my brothers wouldn't let me near their tools and gizmos again. I wondered what sin I had committed, confused because I fixed something essential to our mornings, and all I got in return was disbelief and verbal abuse.

It taught me a valuable lesson: take my knowledge underground, play with Satan, and never tell anyone. Secretly, I continued to fool around with my brothers' Frankenstein-looking test tubes and soldering irons and oscilloscopes, obsessed with electricity and the cool moving visuals it made. I took electronics in high school, veiling my real interest in the subject by claiming that as the only girl in the class, my potential for more dates was greatly enhanced—this somewhat ameliorated my status as class freak.

Later, back in the days of punch cards, I was still fascinated by the visuals, but the shit I had to deal with from the boys in class, now heavy with adoles-cent testosterone poisoning, didn't seem to be worth the time or the time to fuck. I began instead to be overwhelmed by my new desire for a motorcycle. That's more-or-less how I ended up on the so-called Information Superhighway, riding a Ducati instead of a more "powerful" Hog, or an ultra-fast Japanese crotch rocket. I adore its nervous, high-pitched whine, and it is good to my thighs as they wrap around its warm, vibrating engine. I still keep my knowledge veiled from the boys, not so much because I'm afraid of their uncontrollable and bloody little primate urges for domination, but because they are rarely worth the effort.

designers
Stephen Shackleford
Jan C. Almquist

photographer
James B. Abbott

art director
Jan C. Almquist

design company
Allemann Almquist
& Jones

country of origin
USA

work description
Front covers and spreads
from a two-part 1993
Annual Report for The
Franklin Institute Science
Museum

dimensions
210 x 290 mm
8¼ x 11⅜ in

2

In 1934, The Franklin Institute opened a museum with the new idea of "learning by doing," using interactive exhibits. When the Mandell Futures Center and Tuttleman Omniverse Theater opened in 1990, the Museum took another step forward, presenting the science and technology of the 21st century—technology that is currently shaping our lives—in informative, engaging, and entertaining ways.

Almost 1,000,000 people visit the Institute each year. Using interactive videodisks, computer games, demonstrations and interactive displays, science is a lively art at The Franklin Institute.

The Strategic Plan calls for another new look at how the Museum is organized and for the redesign and renovation of almost every Institute exhibit. Exhibits in the Science Center

Museum Visitors	
Groups	155,748
Individuals	834,127
Camp-In Overnight Program	15,000
Facility Rentals	30,000
Workshops	2,000
Total	**1,036,875**

will be expanded and organized around broad themes of basic science—life science; earth and the environment; transportation; and space and astronomy. An expanded traveling exhibition gallery will enable the Institute to accommodate larger special exhibits.

The Mandell Futures Center will focus on two areas of rapidly changing technology—biotechnology and information technology. The information technology exhibit, "Inside Information," is scheduled to open to coincide with the 50th anniversary of the ENIAC computer in 1996.

A renewed focus on evaluation will provide guidance in developing these new initiatives. Key criteria for future growth are enhanced staff training, expanded family programming, and a commitment to continuous quality improvement and to serving a diverse public.

The Franklin Institute will continue its proud tradition of

meeting the needs of a changing community. Exhibits and pro-

grams will be reorganized, refurbished, and reinvented with a

focus on new technologies and the complex issues they raise.

Programs for recognizing scientific excellence are critical in building excitement and interest in science and take place on many levels. For students, the Institute coordinates the region's largest science fair and works to help girls achieve science merit badges. Scholars and inventors have been recognized through Franklin Institute award programs since 1825. Through the Bower Award and Prize for Achievement in Science, founded in 1988, the Institute conducts an international search to identify a distinguished scientist to receive one of the largest American cash prizes in science.

In 1991, The Journal of The Franklin Institute will be reissued as The Journal of The Franklin Institute: Engineering and Applied Mathematics. A second journal, Technology: The Journal of The Franklin Institute, will also be issued in 1994.

Scientists

Bower Award	300 reviewers	200 participants
Scholarly Journals	500 subscribers	
Symposia, lectures	1,000 attendees	
Science and Arts Committee	50 members	

These activities fulfill an important and unique aspect of the Institute's mission, providing opportunities for students, visitors, and educators to interact with scientists whose contributions are shaping our world and our future.

Recognizing scientific excellence and promoting scientific scholarship have been hallmarks of The Franklin Institute since 1825. These efforts will be strengthened by the year 2000.

157

designer
Kees Nieuwenhuijzen

country of origin
The Netherlands

work description
Front cover, title page,
and spread from *The
Low Countries*, for the
Flemish-Netherlands
Foundation "Stichting
Ons Erfdeel"

dimensions
175 x 234 mm
6⅞ x 9¼ in

THE LOW COUNTRIES

ARTS AND SOCIETY IN FLANDERS
AND THE NETHERLANDS
A YEARBOOK

1994·95

Published by the

Flemish-Netherlands Foundation 'Stichting Ons Erfdeel'

(Photo by Michiel Hendryckx)

attention to one aspect that is often neglected or undervalued: Koolhaas' unconventional use of materials. He uses steel sections next to debarked tree trunks, yellow travertine next to roughly worked concrete. All materials are of equal value to the artist, wrote Adolf Loos in 1898, adding that the cladding was more important than the construction which held it in place, and that textiles are the common origin of both architecture and clothing. A particularly clear illustration of this thesis is the Kunsthal's auditorium, which is separated from the surrounding space by a thick curtain. When the auditorium is not in use, the curtain is kept open; when it is rolled up the rising hem gives it the elegance of an evening gown. The architect noted for his conceptual rigour has here produced an especially tactile building. Outside, the walls and roofs are covered with semi-transparent corrugated sheets. They reveal what usually remains unseen: the skeleton of the wall, the movement of the lift – but they conceal the windows. In the evening when artificial light projects the windows onto the corrugated sheets, the effect is unearthly.

PAUL VERMEULEN
Translated by John Rudge.

The designs marked with an asterisk have not been built.
An exhibition of the work of OMA will be held at the Museum of Modern Art in New York at the end of 1994. On this occasion the book *Small, Medium, Large, Extra Large* (a survey of the history of OMA) will be presented.

FURTHER READING

Rem Koolhaas – *Office for Metropolitan Architecture*. In: Architecture and Urbanism, 217, October 1988.

OMA, HANS VAN, *Rem Koolhaas, Architect* (texts in Dutch and English). Rotterdam, 1990.

F

rom

Gazettiers to Newspaper Groups:

The Press in Flanders

At the time of Belgium's independence in 1830, public life in Flanders was completely gallicised. The Flemish middle classes, those who could afford a daily newspaper, read mainly French publications. Flemish newspapers had a very small share of the market, and in any case appeared only two to three times a week. This weak position contrasts sharply with the flourishing beginnings of the Flemish press in the seventeenth century. In the Spanish Netherlands most publications were in Dutch, and the Flemish press set the standard for Europe.

The Flemish press before Belgian Independence

The development of the first Flemish newspapers during the rule of Albert and Isabella (1598-1633) had much to do with the fact that Flanders had many printers of renown. The first gazettiers were, after all, also printers. The first gazettier in the Southern Netherlands to be granted a licence to publish a newspaper was Abraham Verhoeven, with *Wekelicke Tydinghe* (Weekly News, 1629-1631). Two other Antwerp gazettiers were also given permission to publish newspapers. Other licences were granted to Flemish gazettiers in Ghent, Bruges and Brussels. At that time Dutch was a lively, cultural language which was spoken in the highest circles. Naturally, there was no freedom of the press under the Ancien Régime. The press was subject to censorship and was the servant of those in power at the time.

The lead which the Flemish press had built up under Spanish rule (1555-1713) was lost during the Austrian period (1713-1792). Many 'enlightened' journalists of liberal ideas fled from France and came to Flanders, where they were able to resume their activities under the 'enlightened' Austrian rulers. The ideas of the French Enlightenment had enormous impact, and French became the language of culture. More and more French language newspapers were launched in Brussels. During the period of French rule (1792-1814) French became the language of society and the upper classes abandoned Flemish for French. French-language newspapers increasingly drove out those in Flemish. During the Napoleonic period, a sort of linguistic

Since 1987 we have designed and
managed virtually every aspect of ADT's
visual communications strategy, including
its last six annual reports.

ADT is the largest electronic security and
vehicle auction services company in the
world. Its annual report is aimed primarily
at its shareholders in Europe and North

America, and its customers in these
regions. The emphasis shifted in 199
when ADT changed its listing from
London to New York. Since then we
have identified the language to which
the audience there respond.

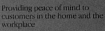

Providing peace of mind to
customers in the home and the
workplace

designers
Simon Browning
Mason Wells

photographer
Tomoko Yoneda

art directors
Ian Cartlidge
Adam Levene

design company
Cartlidge Levene Limited

country of origin
UK

work description
Spread from a brochure
for Cartlidge Levene
Limited

dimensions
295 x 420 mm
11⅝ x 16½ in

160

1993 annual report we worked r client's team to define the objective: to portray ADT as a er-oriented organisation leading icle auctions and security services s. Our design emphasises ADT's on to customer service by ng its close relationships with from major banks to homeowners.

We managed every aspect of the report including art directing the photography across the US, having proofs read in Florida via satellite link and overseeing the production run of 90,000. For the interim report we split the printing between the UK and the US and ran both jobs simultaneously.

Our work with ADT is wide-ranging: from annual reports for Belize Holdings Inc., of which ADT's Michael Ashcroft is also Chairman, to the signage, stationery and student uniforms for the ADT City Technology College in London.

Document specification
Format 21.5 x 28.0cm
52 pages
90,000 copies

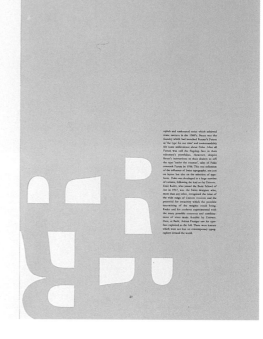

designer
Jason Carr

college
The Surrey Institute of
Art & Design, Farnham

country of origin
UK

work description
Spreads proposed for
Baseline magazine

dimensions
267 x 360 mm
10½ x 14⅛ in

*'i am of the opinion that it is possible to develop
an art largely on the basis of mathematical thinking'*

*'concept should be expressed with greatest
economy - optically not phonetically'*

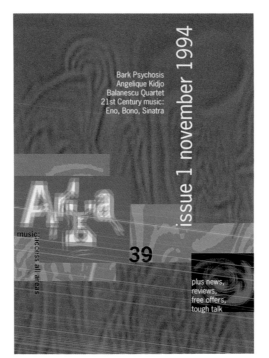

Bark Psychosis
Angelique Kidjo
Balanescu Quartet
21st Century music:
Eno, Bono, Sinatra

issue 1 november 1994

Area

music: across all areas

39

plus news,
reviews,
free offers,
tough talk

designer
Viviane Schott

college
The Surrey Institute of
Art & Design, Farnham

country of origin
UK

work description
Cover and spread from
Area 39, a magazine
project covering
experimental music,
design, and multimedia

dimensions
210 x 297 mm
8¼ x 11¾ in

Together in electric dreams

Why is Brian Eno fascinated by Joe Cocker?

Owired communities around the futuristic campfire
And what's the connection between Bono, Sinatra and Jim Reeves?

In the second of our articles on music in the 21st century,
David Toop looks to a future of sonic collage

What was Elvis doing in a Las Vegas hotel with Mixmaster Morris

Initially, it was about "the city as lover", the relationships possible with places
as much as with people

designers
Mark Diaper
Rachael Dinnis
Mike Davies
Domenic Lippa
Marcus "mad dog" Doling
Jann Solvang

design company
Lippa Pearce Design
Limited

country of origin
UK

work description
Front cover and spreads
from *The Downlow*, the
Hip Hop magazine

dimensions
210 x 297 mm
8¼ x 11¾ in

164

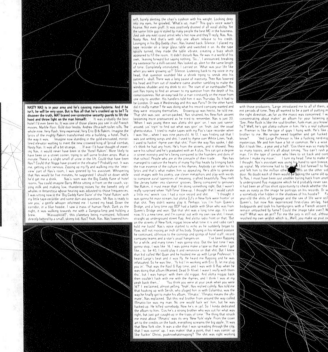

STAIN.

less meets Coolio.

Interview Boy's West Coast Finest Rapper who claims: I knew your Queen when she was working at the K-Mart in Compton and we called her 'Q'. COOLIO has been under the skin of West-Coast Hip-Hop since it began. He was brought up in Compton, became a member of the Crips - and a Krack addict. He learnt his trade on the streets, which he came to know intimately, initially by-passing the recording studios of the district. You could say his background is typical of just another everyday Gangsta Rapper at the start of his career. But Coolio doesn't want to use this time to establish himself. Maybe it's because he knows the streets all too well. His debut album for rapping Buy, 'It Takes A Thief', skips in and around that dark territory, but never comes off as a fully-fledged Gangsta album. Why's that? "Cos I'm a realist, man. I'm a reality Rapper." Coolio tells me. 'Gangsterism is only a part of my life. I don't see it as the basis of what I do. What I do comes from real Hip-Hop. That's what I'm about. Gangsta Rap is cool, but I'm not really a Gangsta.' As we talk Coolio becomes my guide for a tour of the Hood and what happens there. Now things run and what there is all about. Born with a heart made of celluloid, I'm studying to become a film director and so I listen to Coolio's commentary and visualise what he describes. His words become an outline for the kind of motion-picture I'd like to make, a story that's weird, remarkable and packed full of dramatic system.

Read on now and follow Coolio as he introduces us to the Gangs, Krack, Ugly Bitches...and Pigs.

I've always been known as a Rapper. I only gangbanged for a little while. See, if a muthafucka fucked with me I'd fuck with him. But let me tell you what happened. I met two of the craziest muthafuckas on the planet. Two brothers called Goldie and Tito. These muthafuckas, boy, would walk down the street and kill all the dogs. Your dog - and if they liked it they'd kill it. That was crazy! One day they robbed this muthafucka and because he didn't have any money, they killed him. They hit him in the head with the back end of a hammer. I just saw them putting holes in his skull. It was like, damn nigga! I started to throw up. I'd never seen that shit before. So the next day I moved on. That shit wasn't for me. I learned lookin' at life in a different way. I started to learn more about my history. About how things are really supposed to be. See, when I was gangbangin' we used to hit-fights. Gangban35 might get stabbed, but muthafuckas weren't just killin' each other. For me, Gangs were a necessity. It was for protection. 'Coz I was the only child and I was the only one at home. I didn't have nobody to back me up when I got in trouble. So I just started runnin' with the gangs for protection. But the gang situation is unstoppable. The gangs have been going for 40 years, man. See, the way the Gangs are organized, you're only as strong as the strongest person in your gang. The smartest muthafucka in your gang. If your shit-caller is a stupid ignorant, a do-anything muthafucka, then your gang is gonna be like that. But if you've got a smart calculative muthafucka runnin' your shit, then your gang is gonna be smart too, and your hood will make money. But it's not really all about money. It's for protection and territory. Territory is what it's all about. Don't come over here sellin' your dope in my hood and I might not come in your hood, but if you come over here it's on. And now it's moved over to this Colors thang. When it started it wasn't really about Colors. It was just muthafuckaz kickin' it. There wasn't any Bloods, it was all Crips. Crip actually. It originally stood for Consolidated

Trouble

Independent Party. It was a southern Californian division of the Black Panthers. Then something happened at a party. I think some people got killed, and the Crips were blamed. So these muthafuckas were like "Fuck the Crips! We gonna beat them!". So that's how it ran and the Bloods were created. For instance, if I killed your brother, you and me are gonna be enemies forever, right? You gonna wanna kill me, right? So this shit has been has been going on for 40 years. The gangs who have been going on the longest time been the Mexican gangs and the Hispanic gangs. They were around before the Crips. But it don't really matter where you're from or who you are. You fight anybody who comes in ya hood. It's all about money and territory. But when I was comin' up, if you was a Crip you would get a pass. But now Crips don't give a fuck about shit. It started off as something positive for a lot of people. But somehow it got twisted. It wanted off as something real, something positive that could have helped my people. But somehow it got twisted and turned into some bull-shit. So all the shit I grew up on and knew turned out to be bull-shit. Because none of that shit is helping anybody. If you're not part of the solution then you're part of the problem. And the gang situation is one big problem. That Gangsteré was bull shit. It lasted three weeks. Actually it lasted the whole summer, but after that, muthafuckas were usually killed again. After they ran out of BBB

shit was on for everybody going on for you only heard about it when the film "Colors" came out. That's what fucked

everything up. Because before "Colors", gangbangin' was only in California. After that film came out, muthafuckaz started bangin' in Kansas and fucked-up places like Nebraska. There's even a gang of White Crips! Places up in the stix, which have no reason what-soever to be fighting are bangin' homie. Hard bangin'. Do or die, brother. Let me tell you about the South. The South is where the slave trade began. They were the last States to stop the slave trade. They saw all the other States didn't have slaves and they thought "Fuck that! We're keepin' our muthafuckin' slaves!". And that's what the Civil War was about. So the Southern Blacks have a lot more history than the other Blacks. Therefore any

THEY'RE PULL SHIT NOW... COOLIO on the Gangs
"Black Coop, White Coop, Fuck the color of his skin, make sure he's one of US."
"Bring Back Somethin' Fo Da Hood"

CO
O
C
O
L
i
O
O
e

165

designers
Alessio Leonardi
Harald Welt

photographer
Frank Thiel

art directors
Uli Hoyer
Guenther Fannei

design company
Meta Design plus GmbH

country of origin
Germany

work description
Front cover and spreads
(center with gatefold)
from *Hauptstadtformat*, a
brochure for Grundkredit
Bank

dimensions
204 x 270 mm
8 x 10⅝ in

Wir engagieren uns deshalb im Interesse und mit breiter Zustimmung unseres Kundenkreises als andere persönlich und einmütig in vielen Bereichen des öffentlichen Lebens. Insbesondere die Förderung von Kunst und Kultur sind Sport finden große Resonanz bei Freunden und Kunden unseres Hauses. Erhebliches Gewicht haben nahezu soziale Belange. Armen wir uns mit Fördermaßnahmen schließen.

Dabei denken wir weit über das eigentlich wichtigste schon kümmer. Denn nur die gesamtgesellschaftlichen Strukturen harmonisieren. Kann die Wirtschaft erfolgreich, muß und **zukunftsorientiert** zuwege.

Über Panoramablick von Potsdamer Platz.

6–7

„Der **Jahrhundertschritt**"...

...ist unsere Aufgabe für

Berlin und Brandenburg.

Die Chancen und Aufgaben der Deutschen Einheit sind ein Jahrhundertschritt an der Schwelle zu den nächsten Jahrtausend.

Die Grundkreditbank sieht sich hier als regionales Unternehmen besonders gefordert und hat die **Herausforderung** im Interesse ihrer Kunden und der Region konsequent angenommen.

Wir sind davon mit zu sein daß... es verstehen die hier ansässigen den gewerblichen Mittelstand, vermögende Privatkunden, die leistungsbewußten Freiberufler und Investoren sind, mit deren wir unsere Hauptstadt und das Umland zu einem prosperierenden Wirtschaftsraum mit einer einmaligen **Metropole** entwickeln werden.

Die seit mehr Jahren in Weg vollbracht wir in der Spitze gewesen Kunden so schnell wie möglich, aber mit Augenmaß und unter Beherrschen der Verantwortung gehen.

Die GKB hat den Schritt in das nächste Jahrhundert getan.

Wolfgang Mattheuer, Maler, Bildhauer und verschiedene Zeitgenossen, ist mit geometrigen eines, daß Kunst und Künstler ihren Beitrag leisten wie die Bildenden Künstler an der Nordostgrenze des Lebens 1493.

Sein „Jahrhundertschritt" 1984 von Mattheuer, Malerei und Im Bezug der Vielseitig-Zeitungen zwischen Angst und Hoffnung deutlich und wurde zu den wenigen wichtigsten Mitgaben für die Straße.

Mit 1990 steht die Skulptur vor dem Eingangsglas der GKB Dresden als einer.

167

designer
Geoff White

art director
Geoff White

design company
Ilex Marketing Graphic
Design Unit

country of origin
UK

work description
Spreads from a brochure
for Teal Furniture

dimensions
210 x 297 mm
8¼ x 11¾ in

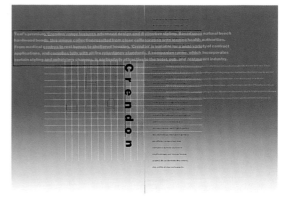

Das von Teal Furniture gepflegte
hohe Qualitätsniveau äußert sich
auch in der Reihe T1000, die
aufgrund ihres ausgezeichneten
Preis-/Leistungsverhältnisses bei
Kommunalbehörden großen Anklang
gefunden hat. Alle Objekte werden
aus erstklassigem Buchenholz
hergestellt und sind entweder in
Naturfarbe oder wunschgemäßen
Beizungen lieferbar. Polster und
Polsterstoffe erfüllen alle geltenden
Flammschutznormen. Unter
Berücksichtigung der von Behörden
und Kunden aus der Freizeitindustrie
entwickelten Vorstellungen wurde
die Reihe T1000 erweitert, um auch
den Bildungs-und Krankenhaus-
sektor anzusprechen.

T1000

Teal Furniture's high production standards
are also applied to the competitively priced
'T1000' range which has proven immensely
popular with local authorities. Manufactured
from the highest quality beechwood, every
item may be supplied in a natural finish or
stained to order. Cover fabrics and
upholstery conform to all current fire
retardancy standards. Acceding to the
demands of leisure and institutional spec-
ifiers, the 'T1000' range has been expanded
to broaden its appeal particularly to the
educational and hospital contract markets.

La qualité standard de production
extrêmement élevée des meubles Teal
est aussi appliquée à la gamme T1000,
aux prix compétitifs, qui a connu un
succès tout particulier auprès des
responsables des collectivités locales.
Fabriqué à partir d'un hêtre de la
meilleure qualité, tout article peut être
livré avec une finition naturelle ou être
teinté sur commande. Ils sont recouverts
de tissus et capitonnés avec des
matériaux qui répondent aux normes
actuelles de l'ignifugation. Satisfaisant
les spécifications de la clientèle des
institutions et des organismes de loisir,
la gamme T1000 a été élargie afin
d'attirer une clientèle plus vaste et en
particulier les marchés des
établissements scolaires et hospitaliers.

designer
Neil Walker

art director
Nicholas Thirkell

design company
CDT Design Ltd

country of origin
UK

work description
Spread from issue one
of *Transformation*, a
publication for Gemini
Consulting

dimensions
237 x 297 mm
9⅜ x 11¾ in

In America, but not yet in continental Europe, the wind went out of shareholder value's sails. The well of junk bond cash ran dry. Our deal-making went the way of John Travolta. We swapped our white disco suits, for Calvin Klein jeans. Icahn and Perelman became sedate businessmen.

Shareholder value has been absorbed into a broader approach. It remains the best representation of the owner's point of view, and that is becoming a precious quality again, at a time when boards are intent on becoming players in the game, rather than decorative wallpaper. And it has found a niche in compensation. If the job of executives is to create value, why not tie their compensation to the value they create for shareholders?

After the first shareholder value wave (there've been others and there will be more) came the new sound of Michael Porter (*fifth generation*). This marked the return of Harvard Business School as the great strategy studio, and a switch from a shareholder, to an industry perspective. The lyrics were tighter, the music more symphonic. The Police replaced the Who. My keyboard soon resembled a helicopter's control panel.

Porter had been a Federal Trade Commission regulator, but he switched sides and, instead of policing oligopolies and monopolies, he began helping companies, and later countries, to shape their industry structure to their own advantage (within those regulatory limits, of course).

"Why does the pharmaceutical industry make money but the OEM tyre business does not?" he asked. "Because there are five forces which determine the profitability of industries" he explained. Executives began buying his records. Some bought the video for their daughters. He also showed that low-cost strategies were not always appropriate, and so demolished 20 years of Boston Consulting Group dogma.

Porter suggested differentiation and focus as strategies and he revamped the clumsy cost structure approach as the "value chain". The look became more formal. Sting rather than Alice Cooper.

My generation welcomed Porter. We thought we had written his book "Competitive Strategy". His approach was refreshing, after leveraged betas, and second and third derivatives. We loved the return of a business perspective, in the tradition of matrix-based models. We were back to civilization. It was music we could play.

It was also an analytical heaven. The five forces model gave us latitude to go study everything: competitors, customers, suppliers, technologies and that magnificent excuse for analytical excess, "potential entrants" (which could include my grandmother, and the Boston Red Sox). Consulting budgets became very large indeed.

Porter's five forces are still useful for capturing industry data, the value chain remains a work horse of strategic analysis, but the generic strategies, and the U-shaped curve have not aged well. They've been branded with the label, "ex post" because they explain what happened but lack predictive power. As Gary Hamel (see below) once uncharitably put it, "Porter's analysis is pure business success-ology. You can study it all you want, but you'll never get there."

From strategic rock 'n' roll to transformational polyphony

After Porter I knew that things would never be the same, so I decided to look for the real me. I left my rock group, and moved to America.

In summer, 1989, I went to a concert in Ann Arbor, Michigan. The band was called Strategic Intent and Core Competencies, and featured C.K. Prahalad, from the University of Michigan, and Gary Hamel, his former student, from the London Business School. The music magazines billed the new band, *sixth generation*.

> "Porter's model is to business success, what Biblical exegesis is to sainthood."

I'd never heard anything like it. The approach was a strange mixture of analytical rigour and mysticism, a blend of old-fashioned heat and oriental influences. Although confused by the multilayered message, I sensed the brilliant strategic prescription. Instantly, I knew they would change my life.

"All the prescriptions of traditional strategic models are fundamentally flawed" Prahalad and Hamel claimed, "because they rely on some kind of segmentation. As a result, each entity fights as a standalone division, rather than as part of an army. That is why the Japanese have destroyed Western rivals over the last 20 years; Cannon versus Xerox, Komatsu versus Caterpillar, and Toyota and Honda versus Ford and GM."

The model uses a botanical metaphor. Each core competency is a root of a tree, and each business, a fruit on the upper branches. The fruit becomes abundant, and succulent, through the nurturing of the roots. The sap rises, promoting growth in the branches, and yielding the lucrative harvest of which business success is made.

"Traditional methodologies are flawed because they pump water directly into the fruit, rather than the roots. How do you feed the roots? By nurturing the core competencies and the business architecture."

I became a disciple. I searched for strategic intent with my clients. I discovered their true metaphor was just that, a metaphor. What mattered was the search. In seeking strategic intent, firms would learn to mobilize their energies. They would begin growing again after decades of contraction. They would reach for higher ground; raise their sights. And, as if by faith healing, their performance would begin to improve.

I felt the power of strange words: like "change management", and "mobilization".

But I was not convinced. "This can't be" I protested. "There must be an analytical key, hidden behind the metaphor". But the more I looked, the more certain I became that there was no secret key. Even so, there was something to this mysticism. The unfathomable Orient was bewitching me. The right side of my brain was taking over the left.

About a year later the world of Market-Focus entered my life (*seventh generation*). My first reaction was that I had heard all this before. "Yeah" I thought, "customer stuff. Old marketing soups, warmed up." It felt like the Rolling Stones attempting a come-back with Mick Jagger at 50.

> "...by jumping several steps down the value chain, we could reinvent businesses and their margins."

But, as I listened to Lynn Phillips and Mike Lanning - the arch-priests of "Building Market-Focused Organizations" - I became intrigued. I had worked a lot with commodity chemical companies (this interest could be traced back to my penchant for weird substances in my rock 'n' roll days), but I had never managed to sell them differentiation. "When you make ethylene oxide, there ain't much you can do, son", a Union Carbide manager had told me.

Phillips and Lanning thought otherwise. And they were right. We invented a strange verb: to "decommoditize". We learned that by jumping several steps down the value chain, we could reinvent businesses and their margins.

Our market-focus workshops developed a following. Companies embarked, with us, on quests for new Value Propositions. We invented "on-line strategy" - making up stuff right there, in front of clients and their customers. I discovered the power of live improvisation - creating business success in collective jam sessions. And because clients saw it unfold in front of their eyes, it was hard for them to discount, or ignore. "Change management" and "mobilization" were back, in their second incarnation.

It was time for my mid-life crisis. I had survived, more or less intact, seven strategic generations. I had moved from my piano, to electronic orchestras; from carefully crafted singles, to unbridled, live improvisations. I'd been shaken to my analytical foundations many times, and been confused

12

13

169

designers
Simon Browning
Yumi Matote

photographer
Richard J. Burbridge

art director
Adam Levene

design company
Cartlidge Levene Limited

country of origin
UK

work description
Front covers from *Visions*
and *Focus*, a two-part
recruitment brochure for
Shell International

dimensions
210 x 297 mm
8¼ x 11¾ in

Visions

There is one industry which, above all others, influences the lives, cultures, economies and politics of all
nations. It offers graduates the broadest possible range of intellectual and managerial challenges.
It promises – and more importantly delivers – the prospect of a truly international future. It is quick to
recognise achievement and always promotes ability. Yet, to graduates, it remains one of the great enigmas.

Focus

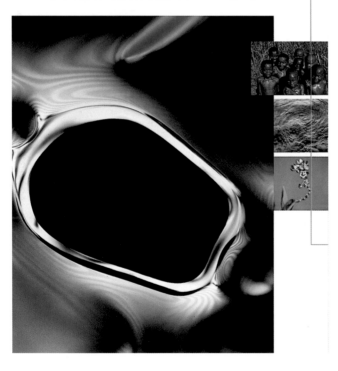

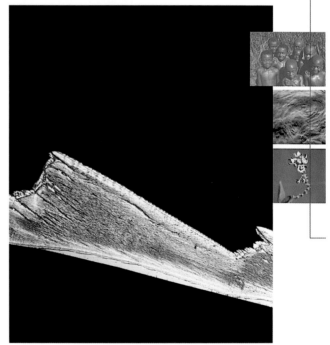

designers
Simon Browning
Helge Kerler
Yumi Matote

photographers
Tomoko Yoneda
Library Images

art director
Ian Cartlidge

design company
Cartlidge Levene Limited

country of origin
UK

work description
Spread from a large
format version of *Visions*,
a recruitment brochure
for Shell International

dimensions
297 x 420 mm
11¾ x 16½ in

171

designer
Erik Spiekermann

design company
Meta Design, San
Francisco

country of origin
USA

work description
Front cover and spreads
from *Stop Stealing Sheep*
(self-published)

dimensions
143 x 215 mm
5⅝ x 8½ in

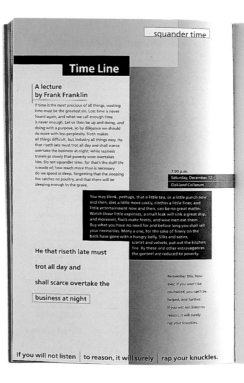

Some of the most pervasive typographical messages have never really been designed, and neither have the typefaces that appear on them. Some engineer, administrator, or accountant in some government department had to decide what the signs on our roads and freeways should look like. This person probably formed a committee made up of other engineers, administrators, and accountants who in turn went to a panel of experts that would have included manufacturers of signs, road safety experts, lobbyists from automobile associations plus more engineers, administrators, and accountants. You can bet there wasn't one typographer or graphic designer in the group, so the outcome shows no indication of any thought toward legibility, let alone communication or beauty. Nevertheless we're stuck with our road signs. They dominate our open spaces, forming a large part of a country's visual culture.

The letterforms on these signs were constructed from simple geometric patterns rather than from written or drawn letterforms because they had to be re-created by signmakers all over the country. It seems our official alphabets are here to stay, even though it is feasible to use other typefaces more suitable for the task.

DIN (Deutsche Industrie-Norm= German Industrial Standard) is the magic word for anything that can be measured in Germany, including the official German typeface, appropriately (and not surprisingly) called DIN-Schrift. Since it's been available in digital form, this face has been picked up by many graphic designers who like it for its lean, geometric lines, features that don't make it the best choice for complex signage projects.

Signage systems have to fulfill complex demands. Reversed type (e.g., white type on a blue background) looks heavier than positive type (e.g., black on yellow), and back-lit signs have a different quality than front-lit ones. Whether you have to read a sign on the move (from a car, for example), or while standing still on a well-lit platform, or in an emergency – all these situations require careful typographic treatment. In the past these issues have been largely neglected, partly because it would have been almost impossible to implement and partly because designers chose to ignore these problems, leaving them up to others who were simply weren't aware that special typefaces could help improve the situation.

Multiple master typefaces (see pages 109–111) like Minion and Myriad can be tuned to every lighting condition and production specification. The PostScript™ data generated with these types in drawing and layout applications can be used to cut letters of any size from vinyl, metal, wood, or any other material used for signs.

Soon there will be no more excuses for badly designed signs, whether on our roads or inside our buildings.

A DIN-Schrift, reversed out.
B Type on back-lit sign suffers from radiant light.

C More explicit letter shapes help (n is more oval, i-dots are round).
D But still, backlighting presents a problem.

E The type has to be just a little lighter, so that finally ...
F It is more legible than in example B.

Köln | Köln | **Köln**

D | E | F

While driving on freeways isn't quite as exhausting as running a marathon (mainly because you get to sit down in your car), it requires a similar mind-set. The longer the journey, the more relaxed your driving style should be. You know you're going to be on the road for a while, and it's best not to get too nervous, but sit back, keep a safe distance from the car in front of you, and cruise.

Long-distance reading needs a relaxed attitude, too. There is nothing worse than having to get used to a different set of parameters every other line: compare it to the jarring effect of a fellow motorist who suddenly appears in front of you, having jumped a lane just to gain twenty yards. Words should also keep a safe, regular distance from each other, so that you can rely on the next one to appear when you're ready for it.

The tricky thing about space is that it is generally invisible and therefore easy to ignore. At night you can see only as far as the headlights of your car can shine. You determine your speed by the size of the visible space in front of you.

It used to be a rule of thumb for headline settings to leave a space between words that is just wide enough to fit in a lowercase *i*. For comfortable reading of long lines, the space between words should be much wider. The default settings in most software vary these values, but the needed 100 percent word space seems just fine for lines of at least ten words (or just over fifty characters). Shorter lines always require tighter word space. (More about that on the following page).

The way to wealth

If time be of all things
the most precious, wasting
time must be the greatest
prodigality; since lost time is
never found again; and what
we call time enough always
proves little enough. Let us
then be up and doing, and
doing to a purpose, so by
diligence we should do more

If time be of all things
the most precious, wasting
time must be the greatest
prodigality; since lost time is
never found again; and what
we call time enough always
proves little enough. Let us
then be up and doing, and
doing to a purpose, so by
diligence we should do more

A lowercase *i* makes
a nice word space
for headlines. Short
lines should have
modest space
between the words.

123

designer
John O'Callaghan

college
Ravensbourne College
of Design and
Communication,
Chislehurst

tutor
Barry Kitts

country of origin
UK

work description
Spreads from a proposed
monthly digest of the
weekly magazine The New
Scientist

dimensions
210 x 297 mm
8¼ x 11¾ in

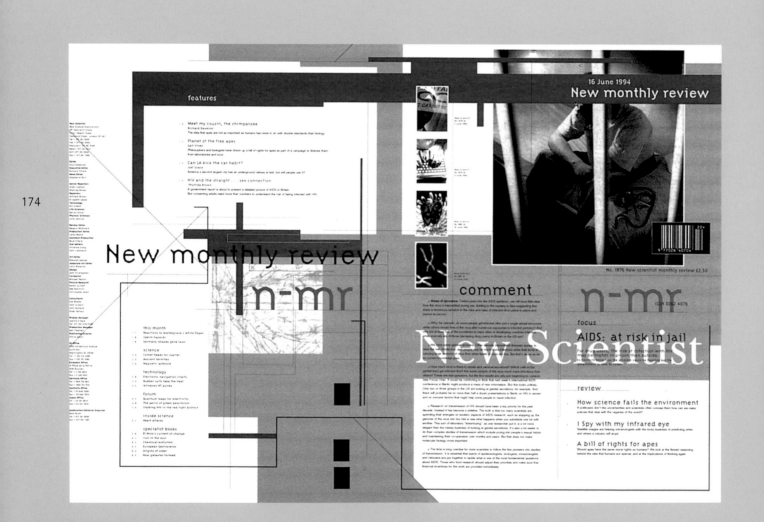

For Britain's hard drug users, even the shortest jail sentence could be life-threatening.

Among drug users, the risk of infection with HIV may be higher in prison than in the outside world. Ex-convicts know how the problem could be tackled but the government is slow to listen.

Most of the 100,000 or so people who inject drugs in this country end up in prison at some point in their lives.

This year alone, some 12,000 of them will be put behind bars. In theory, with their liberty gone, this large group should be safe from the dangers of using drugs and the high risk of contracting HIV that goes with sharing needles and syringes.

But the reality appears to be very different. Interviews conducted by New Scientist with ex-prisoners and with researchers confirm that many drug users do not lose access to drugs inside prison but instead face the risk that they used to avoid becoming infected with HIV.

HIV: high risk behind bars

focus one

designer
P. Scott Makela

photographers
P. Scott Makela
Rik Sferra
Alex Tylevich

art director
P. Scott Makela

design company
Words and Pictures for
Business and Culture

country of origin
USA

work description
Front cover and spreads
from a catalog/prospectus
for Minneapolis College
of Art and Design

dimensions
215 x 292 mm
8½ x 11½ in

MCAD
students are curious, experiment

INVENT, DISCOVER, WORK HARD, BE THEMSELVES, REACH FOR THE STARS. THEIR DETERMINATION AND CURIOSITY HEAT UP THE STUDIOS AND LIGHT THE LABS AT THE MIDNIGHT HOUR. "THE STUDENTS HAVE AN INTERNAL NECESSITY TO MAKE ART AND A GREAT RESPECT FOR ART." *HAZEL BELVO, CHAIR, FINE ARTS DIVISION.* Students come to MCAD from many different backgrounds and experiences, from coastal cities, urban centers and rural towns across the United States and in twenty foreign countries, including Japan, Thailand, Italy and Norway. They come from high school, community colleges, former jobs and former lives. They are committed to their art and their future role as artists and designers in society, and are highly motivated, culturally aware, and ready to take a stand on issues important to them. Passionate about their education, their central mission is to make sense of their experience. **"WE HAVE A ROMANTIC VISION THAT WE ARE MAKING A CHANGE IN THE WORLD. WE ARE ARTISTS WHO ARE VERY SOCIALLY INVOLVED, PARTICIPATING IN SOMETHING BIGGER THAN JUST COMING TO CLASS OR HAVING PIECES IN A SHOW."** *IVAN NUNEZ '90, FINE ARTS, MARACAIBO, VENEZUELA.* **"GOING TO ART SCHOOL IS ABOUT BECOMING CAREFUL VIEWERS. THE MORE ATTENTION WE PAY TO OUR SURROUNDINGS, THE MORE WE CAN LEARN FROM AND APPRECIATE THEM."** *MARIAM STEPHAN, FINE ARTS, PITTSBURGH, PENNSYLVANIA.* **"THERE ARE SUCH TALENTED AND KNOWLEDGEABLE PEOPLE HERE — STUDENTS, TEACHERS, STAFF, EVERYONE. THERE'S INTELLECTUAL DISCUSSION EVERYWHERE, DISCUSSION ABOUT THE ARTS, CHOICES WE MAKE, HOW YOU LIVE YOUR LIFE."** *ROSEMARY RISKIN '93, FINE ARTS, MINNETONKA, MINNESOTA.* MCAD teachers — filmmakers, photographers, graphic designers, fine artists — bring the riches of their own work to the classroom. Their connections sometimes lead to internships, artist apprenticeships and jobs for students. Most of MCAD's faculty have advanced degrees in their fields from the nation's top graduate programs. Students cite faculty as one of MCAD's greatest strengths, not only for their talent and teaching skills, but also because they're such great people. **"MY TEACHERS HAVE BEEN JUST INCREDIBLE! THEY HAVE HELPED ME FOCUS ON WHAT I WANT AND THE DIRECTION I WANT TO GO. THEY HAVE ENCOURAGED ME TO TRY DIFFERENT THINGS — TO GO OUT THERE AND GET MY HANDS DIRTY."** *HEATHER PALMER, FOUNDATION STUDIES, STUDIO CITY, CALIFORNIA.* **"THE INSTRUCTORS ARE SO COMMITTED TO THEIR COURSES AND THEIR STUDENTS THAT IT DEVELOPS A SENSE OF COMMITMENT IN YOU."** *EDMUND ASHLEY, FOUNDATION STUDIES, PORTLAND, MAINE.* Visiting artists stimulate the MCAD environment by teaching courses, giving critiques and public talks and showing their work. Recent visitors included environmental artists Helen Mayer Harrison and Newton Harrison, graphic designer Anthon Beeke from Holland, and photographer Annie Leibovitz. Alumni frequently visit classes to answer your questions about work opportunities in the visual arts and how to prepare for specific careers.

Facilities

Computer Center

Computers are powerful tools that enable designers and artists to explore visual solutions to assignments and production works. They also expand creative horizons and amplify imagination and visual exploration. Although computers make it possible to view more alternatives with great speed, the final image must be the product of a skilled artist's mind and spirit. Computers are utilized by MCAD students in all areas of study. Classes in the Design major incorporate the use of computers in graphic design, package design, furniture, and interactive design. Media Arts students use computers for video editing, electronic photography, and sound composition. 3D modeling programs are applied to sculpture projects; painting and drawing students explore the large array of color painting and illustration software. Computers at MCAD are not just a technical tool, they are a medium for creative expression.

Whether your interest lies in image composition, digital media (video, sound and photography), color painting, 3D modeling and animation, or graphic design and illustration, MCAD's Computer Center puts at your fingertips an incredible range of the latest hardware and software. Color painting and image composition needs are met from our collection of eight paint programs. You can choose from four animation programs, seven drawing and illustration programs, eleven 3D design and modeling programs, three image manipulation programs, four page design and related applications and dozens of other specialized pieces of software. There are plenty of spaces (more than 120 work-

designer
P. Scott Makela

photographers
P. Scott Makela
Rik Sferra
Alex Tylevich

art director
P. Scott Makela

design company
Words and Pictures for
Business and Culture

country of origin
USA

work description
Spread from a catalog/
prospectus for
Minneapolis College
of Art and Design

dimensions
215 x 292 mm
8½ x 11½ in

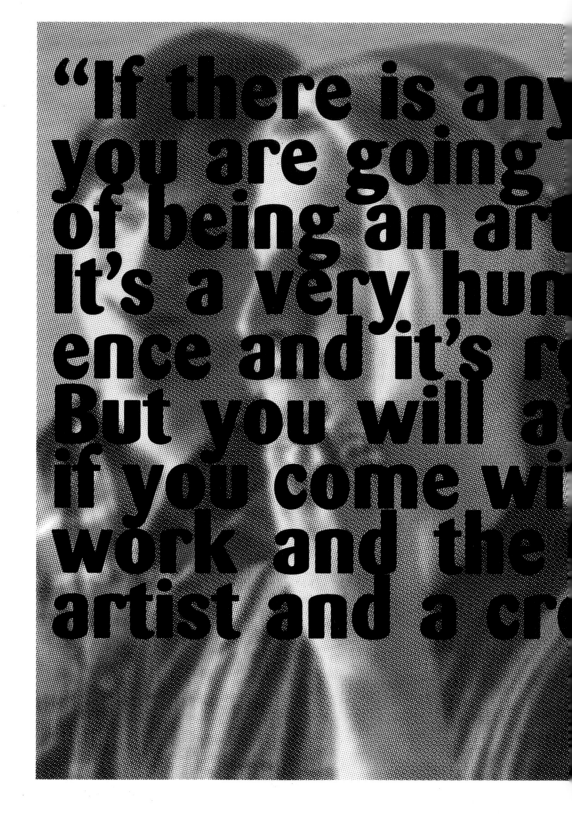

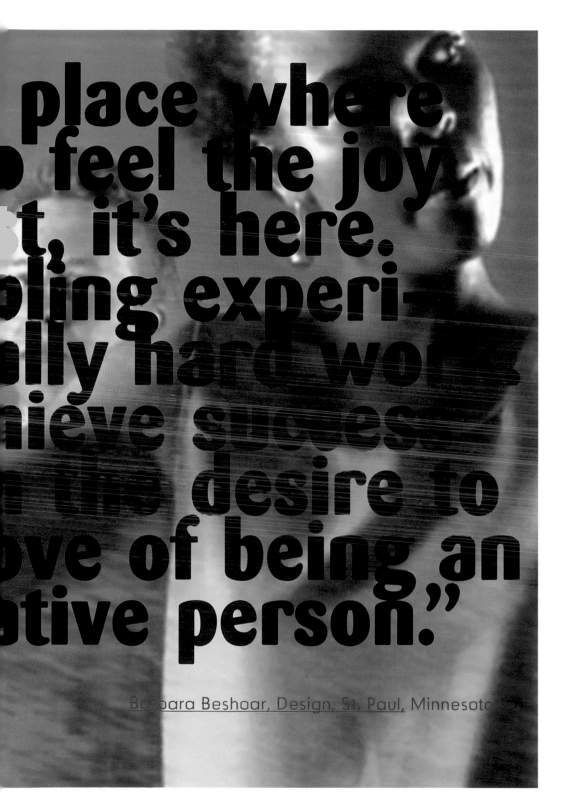

place where
feel the joy
it's here.
ling experi-
lly hard wo
ieve succes
desire to
ve of being an
tive person."

Barbara Beshoar, Design, St. Paul, Minnesota

designer
Denise Gonzales Crisp

college
California Institute of
the Arts

country of origin
USA

work description
Spreads from *A Sign in
Space*, an interpretation
of a story by Italo Calvino

dimensions
270 x 340 mm
10⅝ x 13⅜ in

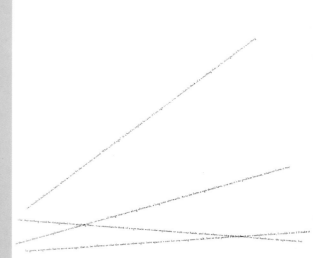

w things were different,
wever, because the world
I mentioned, was
ginning to produce an
mage of itself, and in
everything a form was
we already began to
beginning to correspond to a
realize that the
unction, and forms of that
world's forms had been
ime, we believed, had a long
uture ahead of them
temporary up until
them, and that they
instead, we were wrong;
would change, one by
ake, to give you a fairly
one. And this awareness
cent example, the
inosaurs), and therefore in
certain annoyance with
his new sign of mine you
ould perceive the
nfluence of our
ew way of looking
t things, call it
tyle if you like,
hat special way
hat everything
ad to be, there,
n a certain
ashion, I must say
was truly
atisfied with it,
and I no longer
egretted that
first sign that had
been erased,
because this one
seemed vastly more
beautiful to me.
But in the duration

of that galactic year

was accompanied by a
the old
images, so
that even
their memory
was
intolerable. I
began to be
tormented by a
thought: I had left
that sign in space,
that sign which had
seemed so beautiful and
original to me and so
suited to its function,
and which not, in my
memory,
seemed
inappropriate, in all its
pretension, a sign chiefly
of an antiquated way of
conceiving signs and of my
foolish acceptance of an
order of things I ought to
have been wise enough to
break away from in time. In

other words, I
was ashamed of
that sign which
went on through
the centuries,
being passed by
worlds in flight,
making a
ridiculous
spectacle of itself
and of me and of
that temporary way
we had had of seeing
things. I blushed
when I remember it
(and I remembered it
constantly), blushes
that lasted whole
geological eras: to
hide my shame I
crawled into the
craters of the
volcanoes, in remorse I
sank my teeth into the
caps of the glaciations
that covered the
continents. I was
tortured by the
thought that Kgwgk
always preceding me
in the
circumnavigation of
the Milky Way,
would see the sign

before I could erase it,
and boor that he was, he
would mock me and make
fun of me,
contemptuously
repeating the sign in
rough caricatures in
every corner of the
circumgalactic
sphere. Instead,
this time the
complicated
astral time
keeping was in
my favor.
Kgwgk's
constellation
didn't
encounter the
sign.
whereas our
solar system
turned up
there
punctually
at the end
of the
first
revolution,
so close

I conceived the idea of making
a sign, that's true enough, or
rather, I conceived the idea of
considering a sign a something
that I felt like making, so
when, at that point in space
and not in another, I made
something, meaning to make a
sign it turned out that I really
had made a sign, after all.

s if I make a difference, there were no things to mark, nobody knew what a line was, straight or curved, or even a dot.

In other words, I established it as the first sign ever made

designers
Mark Diaper
Domenic Lippa

design company
Lippa Pearce Design
Limited

country of origin
UK

work description
Front covers and spread
from *Now You See It*, a
series of catalogs for six
performances given at the
South Bank Centre,
London; the cover
material changed each
night (above, from left to
right: corrugated plastic,
latex, paper, corrugated
cardboard, sandpaper,
paper)

dimensions
300 x 250 mm
11⅞ x 9⅞ in

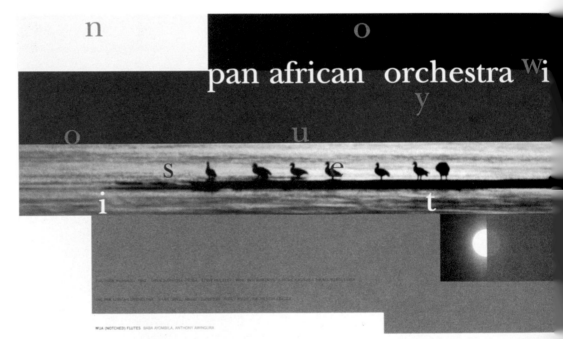

the oren marshall trio
special guest: andy summers

"it has been a great experience recording and working with this marvellous ensemble in the studio. finally to see such an orchestra playing on stage in the west is really good news! this music is the true root of rock and jazz." **andy summers**

10 AUGUST 1994   QUEEN ELIZABETH HALL

designer
Ulysses Voelker

art director
Ulysses Voelker

design company
Meta Design plus GmbH

country of origin
Germany

work description
Front cover case binding
and spreads from
*Zimmermann meets
Spiekermann*; the book
is concertina-folded
allowing text to be seen
through the translucent
paper which is printed
on both sides, published
by Hochschule für Künste

dimensions
213 x 280 mm
8¾ x 11 in

184

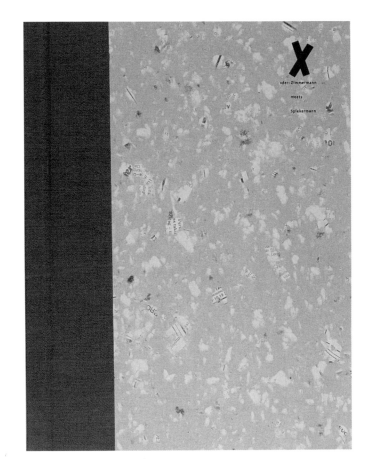

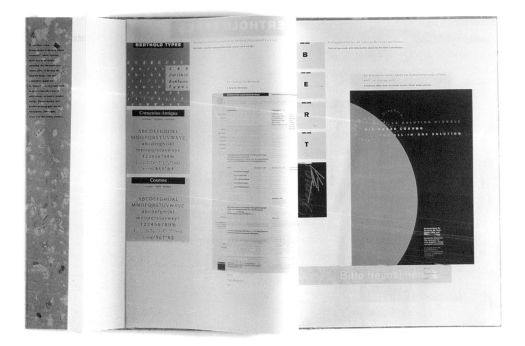

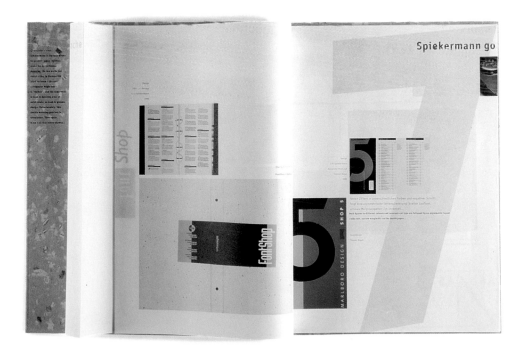

designer
Koeweiden/Postma
Associates

photographer
Marc van Praag

country of origin
The Netherlands

work description
Front cover case binding
and spreads from the
book *Architecten*,
volume 1, for Bis
publishers

dimensions
250 x 300 mm
9⅞ x 11⅞ in

186

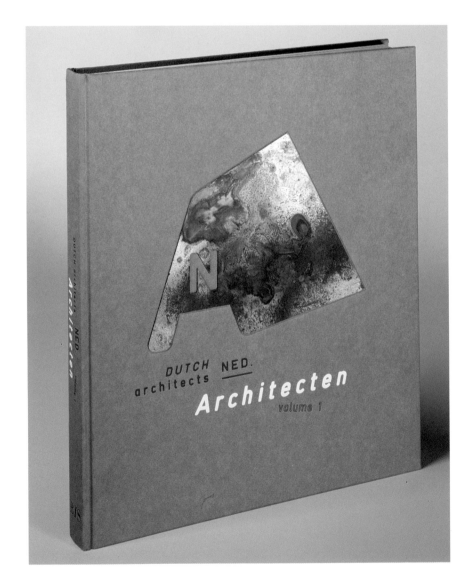

Oving Architekten bv

Architektengroep Duintjer

designer
Loïc Lévêque

photographers
Bobby Adams
Erich Huller
Loïc Lévêque

design company
Loïc Lévêque Design

country of origin
France

work description
Spread and front cover of
an experimental magazine
on Industrial Music (self-
published)

dimensions
276 x 370 mm
10⅞ x 14½ in

Ce pays fonctionne encore comme dans les années 1870, où tout était fondé sur le travail. Pendant plus de 100 ans, ils ont conditionné et éduqué le peuple dans un ordre moral très rigide. Les heures d'ouverture des bars, des restaurants etc, sont réglés sur le temps de travail. Tout ferme tôt, pour que le peuple puisse se lever de "bonne heure" pour travailler. On vit encore le rêve du 19 eme siècle. Si on ne travaille pas, on ne sert moralement à rien. On n'est pas digne, on ne peut pas avoir une place dans cette société. Maintenant, ils ont toute une génération de chomeurs. On nous a tous appris que les chomeurs étaient des lèpreux. C'est pour ça que le pays est dans la merde. Il va falloir qu'on les déconditionne. Il existe cette génération folle de gosses qui ont appris à l'école que leur seul rôle dans la vie c'est de se justifier, donc de travailler. Puis en sortant de l'école, ils se rendent compte qu'il ne travailleront jamais. C'est une génération psychotique. Nous n'y appartenons pas, bizarrement, mais on a grandi ensemble, nous la comprenons. Je suppose qu'ils reconstruiront les maisons des pauvres et tout recommencera, le pays redeviendra celui de Dikens... Vous avez des obsessions ou des intérêts personnels ? Je crois que si un intérêt devient une obsession ça fait très artificiel. C'est devenu chic, d'être obsédé par quelque chose que les autres trouvent dégueulasse.. Certains estiment que la fascination du mal renie toute moralité bourgeoise, mais il me semble qu'aller à l'extrème deviendrait une sorte de snobisme. J'appellerais mes obsessions "fascinations curieuses", pas obsession. Nous sommes très intéressés par les rythmes, en ce moment. Nous sommes des primitifs urbains. On est facsiné par les primitifs ethniques . Je ne dis pas qu'on soit un groupe ethnique, mais on est conscient (comme les musiciens Jajoukas) de cette force primitive. On ne les imite pas, on est des primitifs modernes. Je ne crois pas qu'on essaye de l'être, on est naturel. On n'a pas de propagande, on ne dit pas, voilà ce qu'on fait, voilà ce qu'on est. Qu'on essaye de rendre la musique commerciale, ou qu'on essaye de la rendre bizarre, l'essentiel, c'est que ce soit instinctif, et dans ce sens-là, je crois qu'on est primitif. Je crois

bruit

189

designer
Robert Hunter

college
The Surrey Institute of
Art & Design, Farnham

country of origin
UK

work description
Spread from *Area 39*,
a magazine project
covering experimental
music, design, and
multimedia

dimensions
210 x 297 mm
8¼ x 11¾ in

190

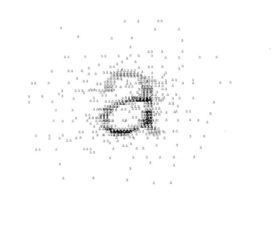

AREA 39 LTD, 45-46 POLAND STREET, LONDON W1V 3DF TEL 071 439 6422 FAX: 071 287 4767

AREA 39 IS AN EXPERIMENTAL MAGAZINE WHICH WILL CONCENTRATE WITHIN THE FIELDS OF FUTURE MUSIC, GRAPHIC DESIGN AND EVOLVING WORLD OF MULTIMEDIA TECHNOLOGY. THE MAGAZINE WILL TRY TO INCOURAGE THE READER TO BECOME AN INVOLVED PARTICI-PANT WITHIN THE CREATIVITY OF THE EDITORIAL LAYOUT AND FEATURES OF THIS NEW EXPERIMENTAL MAGAZINE. AREA 39 WILL BE AVAILABLE TO PURCHASE EVERY MONTH FROM LOCAL MUSIC STORES. THE MAGAZINE WILL INCLUDE ARTICLES ABOUT ELECTRONIC MUSIC. THERE WILL ALSO BE INTERVIEWS WITH WELL KNOW ARTISTS IN THE FIELD OF TECHNO HOUSE DANCE ABIENT AND NOISE. EVERY MONTH AREA 39 WILL BE INFORMING THE READER OF CURRENT ISSUES IN EXCLUSIVE INTERVIEWS WITH THE PEOPLE THAT KNOW. THE MAGAZINE WILL ALSO BE INVOLVED IN INFORMING THE PUBLIC OF THE LATEST DESIGN ISSUES AND FEATURES AN INSIGHT INTO THE GRAPHIC WORLD, WHEATHER (NEW OR RETROSPECTIVE). INTERVIEWS ON GAME PRODUCERS FROM SEGA AND SNES WILL ALSO BECOME A MONTHLY FEATURE WITH VIRTUAL REALITY AND GAME TECHNOLOGY ARE BROUGHT TO YOUR ATTENTION WE INVITE THE WORLD'S MOST CRE-ATIVE GAME PROGRAMMERS TO SHOW HOW IT IS ACHEIVED. IF YOU WOULD LIKE TO ADVERTISE OR BE INVOLVED WITH INTERVIEWS OR WITHIN THE MAGAZINE CONTACT US...

7

designer
Anthony Oram

college
The Surrey Institute of
Art & Design, Farnham

country of origin
UK

work description
Spread from *Area 39*,
a magazine project
covering experimental
music, design, and
multimedia

dimensions
297 x 420 mm
11¾ x 16½ in

designers

Andrew Hall
Stuart Brown

college

Falmouth College of Art

country of origin

UK

work description

Front cover and spread
from *Lizard*, the first
student magazine of
Falmouth College of Art

dimensions

210 x 210 mm
8¼ x 8¼ in

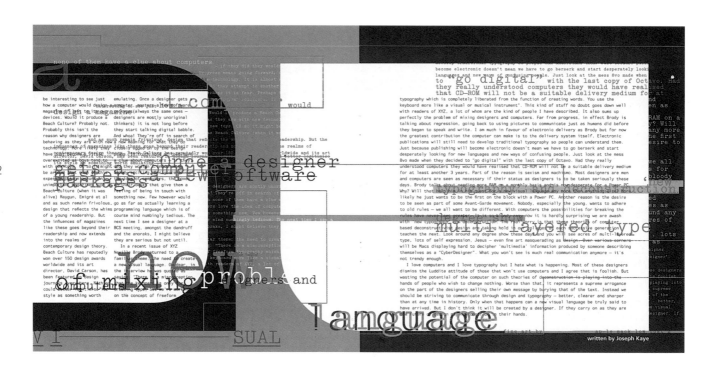

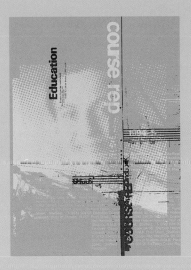

designer
Neil Fletcher

design company
Pd-p

country of origin
UK

work description
Front cover and spread
from the *Course
Representative Handbook*
for the Union of Students,
Sheffield Hallam
University

dimensions
210 x 297 mm
0¼ x 11¾ in

2

Sheffield Hallam University Union of **Students sees
the improving quality and relevancy
of your education as one of its major
priorities. >As a result the Education
Unit is in pl**ace to co-ordinate all
of the Student Unions' educational
and representational work.
In providing support for student
representation at all
levels, raising awareness
of student rights and
**developing a resource base to be used for
the benefit of all students at the University,
the Education Unit.→**

Education Unit
Course Rep Handbook: **Page two**

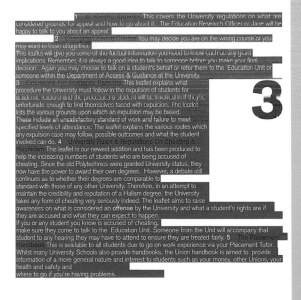

Education Unit Sheffield Hallam University Union of Students sees the improving quality and relevancy of your education as one of its major priorities. As a result the Education Unit is in place to co-ordinate all of the Student Unions' educational and representational work. In providing support for student representation at all levels, raising awareness of student rights and developing a resource base to be used for the benefit of all students at the University, the Education Unit has a strong commitment to achieving these objectives.

Who are we: VP Education: **Jane Whalen**, Education Research Officer: [hoping to appoint shortly], Student Services Administrator **Chris Smalley**, Education Officer. **Heather Ditch.**

Where are we: The Education Unit is based on the top floor of the Nelson Mandela Building, City Campus. You can contact us to make an appointment by: • calling in between 10 pm and 4 pm • ringing up on 534125. • contact us through your Site Union Office. Advice Work Both the Education Research Officer and Jane can offer independent advice and information on a number of academic related problems. As a rep your role may be to speak to us on behalf of a student or to refer the student to see us themselves. For student reference we produce a number of booklets that you may find helpful:

Education Unit
Course Rep Handbook: **Page three**

1 Academic Appeals This covers the University regulations on what are considered grounds for appeal and how to go about it. The Education Research Officer or Jane will be happy to talk to you about an appeal. **2** Changing/Leaving Course You may decide you are on the wrong course or you may want to leave altogether. This leaflet will give you some of the factual information you need to know such as any grant implications. Remember, it is always a good idea to talk to someone before you make your final decision. Again you may choose to talk on a student's behalf or refer them to the Education Unit or someone within the Department of Access & Guidance at the University. **3** Expulsions For Academic Reasons This leaflet explains what procedure the University must follow in the expulsion of students for academic reasons and the procedure a student will be involved in if they're unfortunate enough to find themselves faced with expulsion. The leaflet lists the various grounds upon which an expulsion may be based. These include an unsatisfactory standard of work and failure to meet specified levels of attendance. The leaflet explains the various routes which any expulsion case may follow, possible outcomes and what the student involved can do. **4** University Rules & Regulations On Cheating & Plagiarism This leaflet is our newest addition and has been produced to help the increasing numbers of students who are being accused of cheating. Since the old Polytechnics were granted University status, they now have the power to award their own degrees. However, a debate still continues as to whether their degrees are comparable to standard with those of any other University. Therefore, in an attempt to maintain the credibility and reputation of a Hallam degree, the University takes any form of cheating very seriously indeed. The leaflet aims to raise awareness on what is considered an offense by the University and what a student's rights are if they are accused and what they can expect to happen. If you or any student you know is accused of cheating, make sure they come to talk to the Education Unit. Someone from the Unit will accompany that student to any hearing they may have to attend to ensure they are treated fairly. **5** The Placement Handbook This is available to all students due to go on work experience via your Placement Tutor. Whilst many University Schools also provide handbooks, the Union handbook is aimed to provide information of a more general nature and interest to students such as your money, other Unions, your health and safety and where to go if you're having problems.

3

type itself
type itself

designer
Edward Fella

country of origin
USA

typefaces
various

work description
A double-sided lecture
poster for Neville Brody,
using a visual vocabulary
designed to oppose that
of Brody's

dimensions
279 x 432 mm
11 x 17 in

196

197

designer
David Bravenec

college
California Institute
of the Arts

country of origin
USA

typeface
Dactylo

work description
Typeface formed from
fingerprint fragments
melded with circuit bits,
shown on poster

dimensions
poster
457 x 610 mm
18 x 24 in

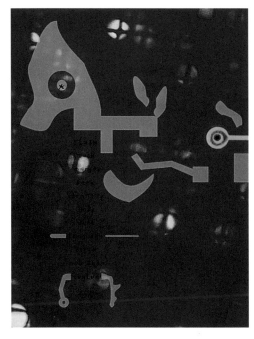

198

designer
Michael Ellot

college
The Surrey Institute of
Art & Design, Farnham

country of origin
UK

typeface
Phutik

work description
Typeface, shown in use on
magazine project

dimensions
page
210 x 297 mm
8¼)(11¾ in

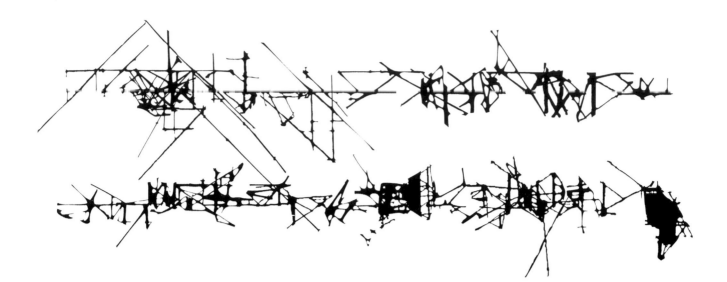

designer
Jason Bailey

college
Royal College of Art,
London

country of origin
UK

typeface
Network

work description
Typeface combining
digital networks with
organic growth

200

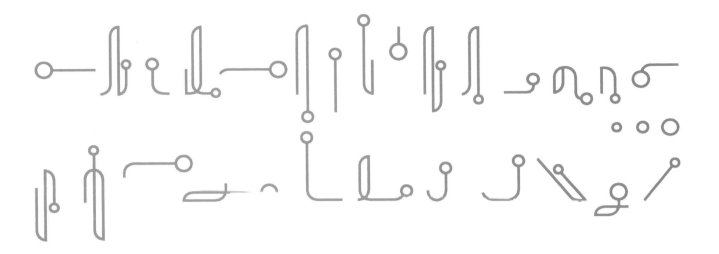

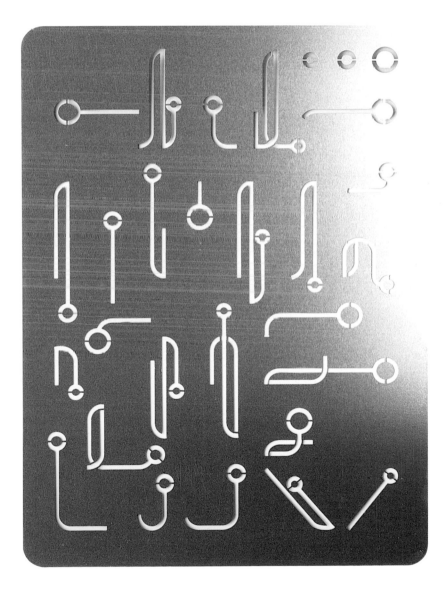

designer
Graham Evans

college
Royal College of Art,
London

country of origin
UK

typeface
Nails

work description
A typeface (shown left cut
out of metal) exploring
the oral/pictorial duality
of language as a written
form: verticals represent
explosive and implosive
sounds, horizontals
represent monothongs/
dipthongs, and the "nail
heads" vary in size
according to sound time

designer
Graham Evans

college
Royal College of Art,
London

country of origin
UK

typeface
Subliminal

work description
A typeface attempting to
visualize a message that
is subliminally received by
smokers who, under
general anesthetic for
surgery, are played a tape
telling them that they
want to give up smoking

dimensions
584 x 414 mm
23 x 16½ in

202

203

designer
Tom Hingston

country of origin
UK

typeface
Metro

work description
Typeface designed for
public information, shown
on advertising poster
(below, right) and on
experimental tickets for
the Metrolink tram
system in Manchester
(below, left)

dimensions
poster
594 x 420 mm
23⅜ x 16½ in

designers
Brigid McMullen
Nina Jenkins

art directors
Brigid McMullen
Martin Devlin

design company
The Workroom

country of origin
UK

typeface
Calculus

work description
Typeface designed for
the Chartered Institute
of Management
Accountants, shown on
front covers of brochures

dimensions
brochure, far left
220 x 310 mm
8⅝ x 12¼ in
others
210 x 297 mm
8¼ x 11¾ in

205

designer
Philippe Apeloig

design company
Philippe Apeloig Design

country of origin
France

typeface
Square

work description
New Year's Card

dimensions
card
180 x 180 mm
7⅛ x 7⅛ in

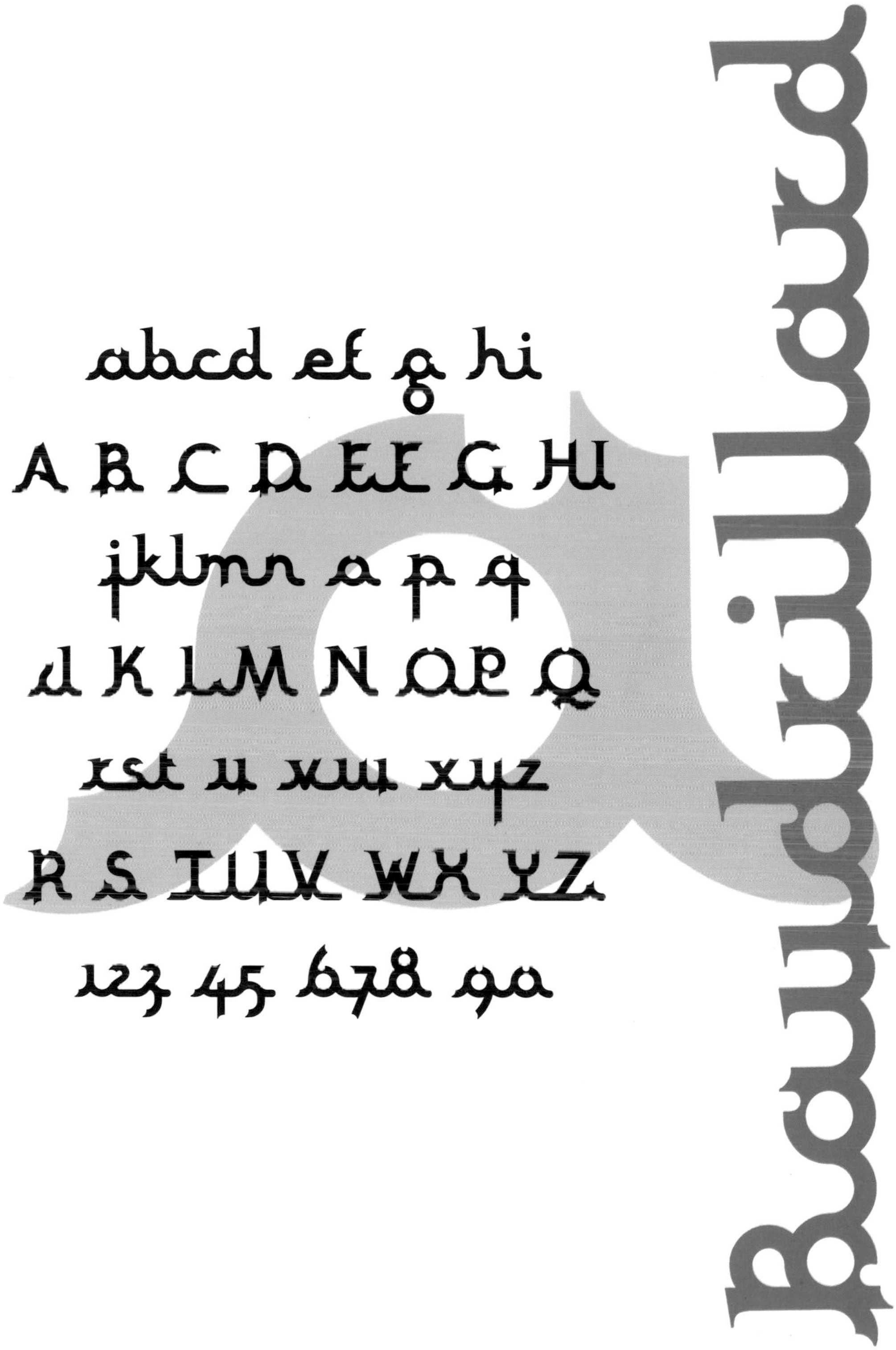

abcd ef g hi

A B C D E E G HI

jklmn o p q

d K LM N OP Q

rst u xuu xyz

R S TUV WX YZ

123 45 678 9a

Baudrillard

designer
Weston Bingham

college
California Institute of
the Arts

country of origin
USA

typeface
Baudrillard

work description
Typeface which
simulates features from
handwritten or hand-
lettered alphabets, but
disregards their original
contexts in favor of
computer generation

ABCDEF
GHIJKLM
NOPQRST
UVWXYZ

MR. KEEDY'S
"GRAPHIC DESIGN (IS) NOW"

designer
Michael Worthington

college
California Institute of
the Arts

country of origin
USA

typefaces
Koo Koo Bloater (above)
Koo Koo Fatboy (center)
Koo Koo Bulemic (below)

work description
Typeface and spread from
Future Context magazine

dimensions
magazine spread
279 x 216 mm
11 x 8½ in

208

ABCDEFG
HIJKLMN
OPQRST
UVWXYZ

abcdef
ghijklm
nopqrst
uvwxyz

ABCDEFG abcdefg
HIJKLMN hijklmn
OPQRST opqrst
UVWXYZ uvwxyz

67890

abcdefg
hijklmn
opqrst
uvwxyz

designer
Richard Shanks

college
California Institute of
the Arts

country of origin
USA

typeface
Cardigan

work description
Typeface designed for
multimedia use, shown on
advertising poster

dimensions
508 x 610 mm
20 x 24 in

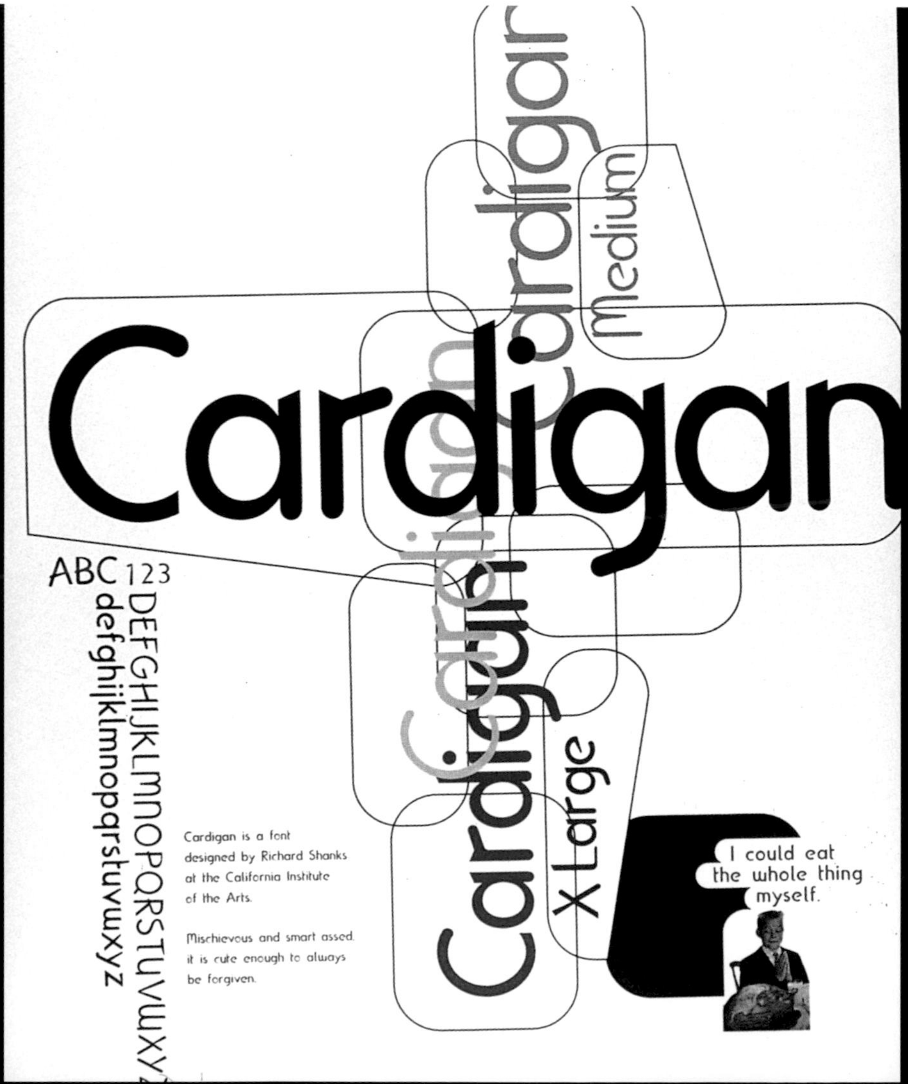

Cardigan

Cardigan Medium

Cardigan X-Large

ABC 123
DEFGHIJKLMNOPQRSTUVWXYZ
defghijklmnopqrstuvwxyz

Cardigan is a font
designed by Richard Shanks
at the California Institute
of the Arts.

Mischievous and smart assed,
it is cute enough to always
be forgiven.

I could eat
the whole thing
myself.

designer
Richard Shanks

college
California Institute of
the Arts

country of origin
USA

typeface
Taxi

work description
Retro-future typeface,
shown on advertising
poster

dimensions
508 x 610 mm
20 x 24 in

taxi

ABCo.

abcdefghijklmnopqrstuvwxyz
ABCDEFGHIJKLMNOPQRSTUVWXYZ

Taxi is a font designed by Richard Shanks

at the California Institute of the Arts
It invokes an appreciation for the past
while signalling a direction for the future.

abcdefgh
stuvwxyz

"Stuck in the suburban Hell
of CalArts Valencia,
I wanted to design a
"city" font, something
as dynamic as all that
hustle hustle and also as charming as a city's rich history." I miss the city

designer
Vivienne Schott

college
The Surrey Institute of Art
& Design, Farnham

country of origin
UK

typeface
Blotter

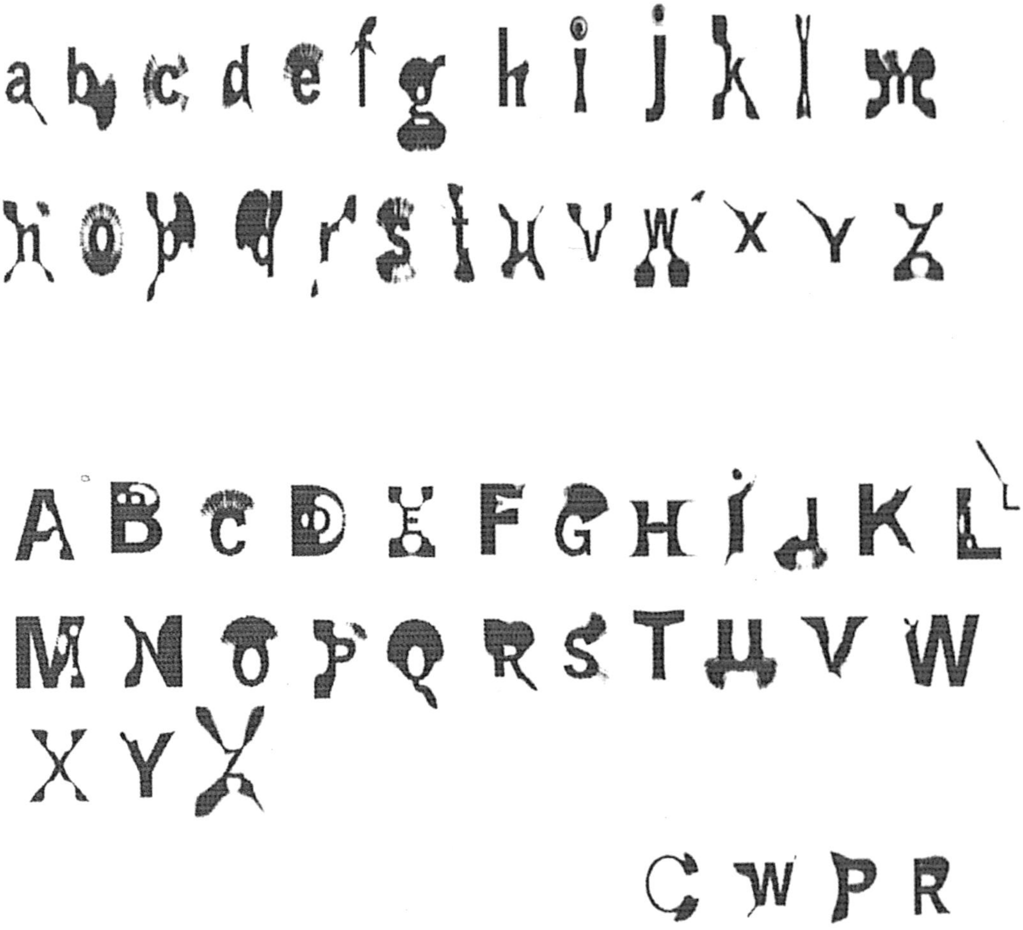

a b c d e f g h i j k l m
n o p q r s t u v w x y z

A B C D E F G H I J K L
M N O P Q R S T U V W
X Y Z

C W P R

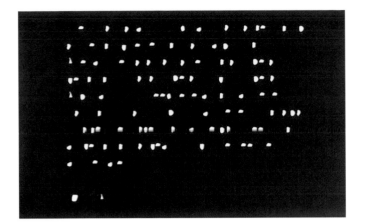

The history of art is simply a history of getting rid
of the ugly by entering into it, and using it.
After all, the notion of something outside of us
being ugly is not outside of us but inside of us.
And that's why I keep reiterating that we're
working with our minds. What we're trying to do
is to get them open so that we don't see things
as being ugly, or beautiful, but we see them just
as they are.

JOHN CAGE

The history of art is simply a history of getting rid
of the ugly by entering into it, and using it.
After all, the notion of something outside of us
being ugly is not outside of us but inside of us.
And that's why I keep reiterating that we're
working with our minds. What we're trying to do
is to get them open so that we don't see things
as being ugly, or beautiful, but we see them just
as they are.

JOHN CAGE

designer
Christian Küsters

college
Yale University School of
Art, Connecticut

country of origin
USA

typeface
Underwater

work description
Typeface shown in three
phases: the negative
underwater, the negative
drying, and the final print

dimensions
432 x 279mm
17 x 11 in

213

type designer
Edward Fella

designer
Rudy VanderLans

photographer
Rudy VanderLans

art director
Rudy VanderLans

design company
Emigre Graphics

country of origin
USA

typeface
Outwest

work description
Poster advertising
typeface

214

dimensions
570 x 830 mm
22½ x 32⅝ in

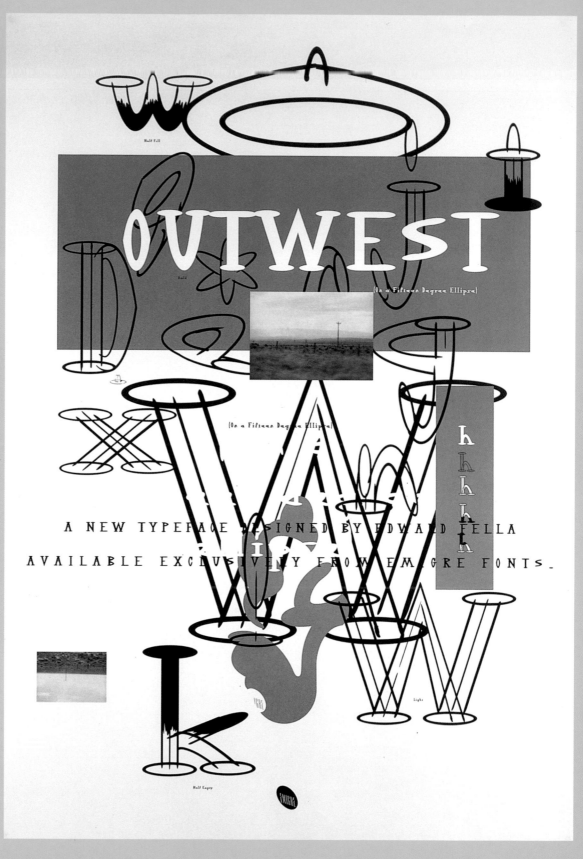

font illustrator
Edward Fella

designers
Gail Swanlund
Rudy VanderLans

art director
Rudy VanderLans

design company
Emigre Graphics

country of origin
USA

typeface
Fellaparts

work description
Poster advertising
typeface

dimensions
570 x 830 mm
22½ x 32⅝ in

215

designer
Conor Mangat

college
California Institute of
the Arts

country of origin
USA

typeface
Stereo Type

work description
Typeface exploring
stereotypical traits of
English and American
typography

dimensions
457 x 610 mm
18 x 24 in

the Bauhaus finally gets the Cal-Look! Dining
heartily on a slice of American car culture,
platelet draws from the existing characters of
Californian license plates to create a whole host
of new opportunities for the typographically-
minded driver. AVAILABLE IN THREE COMPLEMENTARY
FLAVOURS, PLATELET IS NOW AVAILABLE EXCLUSIVELY
FROM EMIGRE FONTS. TO order, call
1-800-944-9021.

abcdefghijklmnopqrstuvwxyzABCDE
FGHIJKLMNOPQRSTUVWXYZ1234567890
#¶@£ƒ$%*b™!&@?~§.

type and design conor mangat, 1994. grateful thanks go to phil baines, rupert bassett, ravensbourne college, and the square and studio mr woody helped a bit too

thin|regular|heavy

designer
Conor Mangat

college
California Institute of
the Arts

country of origin
USA

typeface
Platelet

work description
Typeface derived from the
characters of Californian
license plates, shown on
an advertisement for
Emigre fonts

dimensions
285 x 425 mm
11¼ x 16¾ in

217

designer
Michael Worthington

college
California Institute of
the Arts

country of origin
USA

typeface
Dominatrix

work description
Typeface, shown in use on
advertising poster

dimensions
poster
508 x 813 mm
20 x 32 in

designer
Huw Morgan

country of origin
UK

work description
Ideas for a changeable
typeface, shown in a
sketch book

dimensions
292 x 406 mm
11½ x 16 in

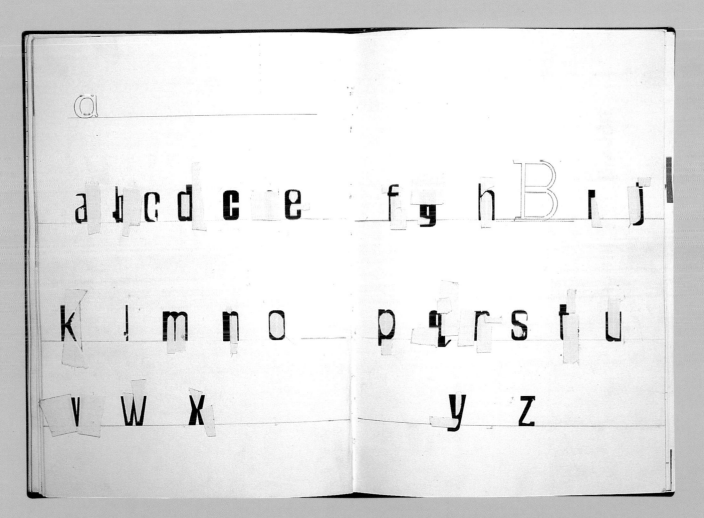

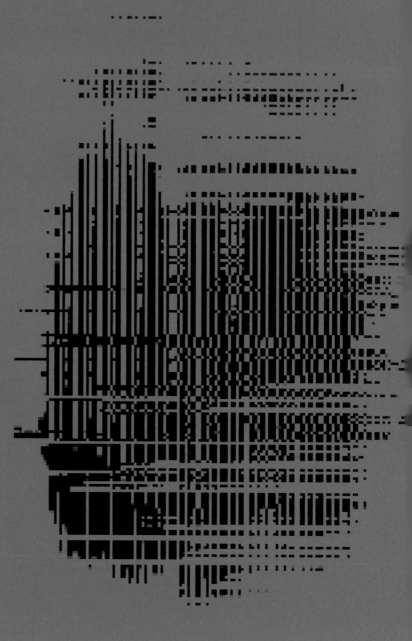

index

Index

List of Colleges

Atelier National de Création
Typographique
Imprimerie Nationale
12 bis rue du Capitaine Ménard
75732 Paris
France

Bath College of Higher Education
Sion Place
Lansdown
Bath BA1 5SF
UK

California Institute of the Arts
24700 McBean Parkway
Valencia
California 91355-2397
USA

Central Saint Martin's College of
Art and Design
Southhampton Row
London WC1B 4AP
UK

Cranbrook Academy of Arts
1221 N. Woodward Avenue
Bloomfield Hills
MI 48303
USA

Ecole Nationale Supérieure des Art
Décoratifs
31 rue d'Ulm
75005 Paris
France

Falmouth College of Art
Woodlane
Falmouth
Cornwall TR11 4RA
UK

London College of Printing and
Distributive Trades
Elephant and Castle
London SE1 6SB
UK

Ravensbourne College of Design
and Communication
Walden Road
Chislehurst
Kent BR7 5SN
UK

Royal College of Art
Kensington Gore
London SW7 2EU
UK

The Surrey Institute of Art
and Design
Falkner Road
Farnham
Surrey GU9 7DS
UK

Utrecht School of the Arts
Boueierbakker Laan 50
3582 VA
Utrecht
The Netherlands

Yale University School of Art
PO Box 2082412
New Haven
Connecticut
06520-8242
USA

Acknowledgments

The Publishers would like to thank
the following people for their help
in producing this book: Nick Bell,
Tony Cobb, Jennifer Harte,
Gabriella Le Grazie, Geoff White,
Karen Wilks for contacting
designers and educational
institutes; Peter Crowther
Associates for producing the
voiceprints reproduced on the
jacket and the chapter openers;
David Murray for photographing
some of the work.

Future Editions

If you would like to be included in
the call for entries for the next
edition of *Typographics* please
send your name and address to:
Typographics, Duncan Baird
Publishers, Castle House, Sixth
Floor, 75-76 Wells Street, London
W1P 3RE, UK. As a collection point
has not yet been finalized, samples
of work should not be forwarded
to this address.